Computer Networks for Distributed Information Systems

Computer
Networks
for
Distributed Information Systems

DIMITRIS N. CHORAFAS

PBI
a petrocelli
book
new york / princeton

621.38
C 551

Library of Congress Cataloging in Publication Data
Chorafas, Dimitris N
    Computer networks for distributed information
systems.
    Includes index.
    1. Computer networks   2. Data transmission
systems. I. Title.
TK5105.5.C484   621.38   80-10440
ISBN 0-89433-105-1

Contents

Introduction

Knowing how to operate large machines or to build elegant systems that provide the most efficient hardware or software is only part of the information problem. The real issue is how to solve business problems by making information work for the people who need it.

The starting point is understanding how information capabilities are received by and delivered to the end users. To do this requires a knowledge of the business—how it operates and what the important issues are.

The implementation process for computers and data communications includes:

1. Gaining management's recognition and acceptance from the beginning.
2. Obtaining a commitment to the tangible and intangible costs of change.
3. Involving the end user in the design of the change (he won't change unless he wants to).
4. Acquiring technologies that match needs and that people will accept.
5. Designing man-machine interfaces and limiting the impact on organizational structures and relationships.
6. Keeping costs lower than the benefits derived.
7. Implementing the change effectively (with the appropriate training and sales effort).
8. Planning the gradual evolution of information technology within the organization.
9. Training the user to the new system and demonstrating cost and benefit in a simple, efficient, understandable manner.

On paper, cost/benefit is easy to demonstrate. The cost performance ratio of computer hardware has improved by a factor of 200 each decade since 1953, or 15 percent a year. Unless new software technology can turn the need from programmer training to training users at intelligent terminals and minicomputer, the advancing hardware technology will lack the understructure on which to build. Indeed, among the factors that contribute to the success of a systems development project the most important is the participation of the primary user.

The success of the system is directly related to the user's involvement. This is often overlooked by management because of the highly technical nature of computer systems and the attitude systems development should be the responsibility of a computer specialist. Often the computer specialist has grand notions that he knows what is "best" for the user forgetting that his job is to satisfy the user by providing him with an efficient system.

There is, however, a rational approach to system analysis that is valid both with computers and with communications networks. The user requirements analysis sets down the user's needs in terms of functional applications and transactions volumes so that an accurate yardstick is available against which to match the applications software capabilities and provide estimates of the needed hardware capabilities. This is written in consideration of the fact that the main object of computing is foresight, insight, analysis, and design. It is neither the automation of numerical calculation, nor the handling of bread and butter accounting data which can be treated more economically through simpler methods.

The principle is just as true as of data processing as it is of data communications. This book has been written with it in mind.

Let me close by expressing my thanks to everyone who contributed in making this book possible: from my colleagues, for their advice; to the organizations I visited in my research, for their insight; and to Eva-Maria Binder, for the drawings and the typing of the manuscript.

Dimitris N. Chorafas

1

Distributed Information Systems

Technology has advanced to the point where computer power is economically available at all levels of company operations. Distributed information systems are tools which enhance the productivity of organizations with widespread operating facilities. Productivity gains can only be expected, however, if system tools are used easily, by authorized individuals, for a variety of purposes, and can be adapted readily as requirements change.

Distributed information systems, DIS, increasingly draw attention, yet have a meaning that is not totally understood. DIS is an evolution from centralized processing, which in turn evolved from "free-standing" modes. Although it combines certain strengths of its two predecessors, DIS is unique in its own right. It represents a break from the past.

The implementation of a distributed information system rests both on Logical and on Physical premises. The logical functions center on the procedural design for channeling the flow of information, and controlling the physical faculty throughout the projected systems configuration. The object of the physical functions is the engineering of the hardware and hard software devices to provide a specific level of capability.

Figure 1.1 outlines the chronological order of development from the information service request to the logical and the physical design phases. The information service request can be motivated by the need for cost reduction in data processing, clerical operations or other sectors, and/or by requests for improving the current information handling service and bringing it nearer to the user.

We shall take factual and documented examples to back up these references.

One Minicomputer per Office

Typically, the information handling service for cost efficiency is centralized, batch oriented, costly, and encounters an inordinate number of errors. Management

Figure 1.1

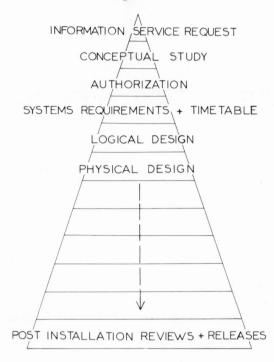

INFORMATION SERVICE REQUEST

CONCEPTUAL STUDY

AUTHORIZATION

SYSTEMS REQUIREMENTS + TIMETABLE

LOGICAL DESIGN

PHYSICAL DESIGN

POST INSTALLATION REVIEWS + RELEASES

needed to do something about this situation, and knew it. It was assisted in opening a new frontier by the system analysts' own realization that new ways were badly needed to master complex information systems.

In the late 1960s information system designers started to realize that software projects could not (and should not) always be behind schedule, taking more memory than planned, costing several times more than the original estimate, and performing less than projected. But it took another ten years to bring into perspective the fact that such results were the direct effect of underestimating complexity: there is no one-dimensional way from systems analysis to programming, but a four-dimensional approach past the architectural level involving noncomputerized procedural design, data base (DB) organization, software design, and hardware engineering. Figure 1.2 gives a snapshot of this organization. We shall return to it later at greater length.

The second vital element in opening the new frontier has been brought about by the cutting edge of technology which made it possible to bring computer power to the workplace at a lower cost than the previous mammoth solutions. Incorrectly called "minicomputers," this generation of information equipment made feasible both the division and the multiplication of computer power. Introduced in the mid-1960s, the minicomputer (based on semiconductors) exploded in the 1970s into three families each with its own market and price range: the maximini (or

Figure 1.2

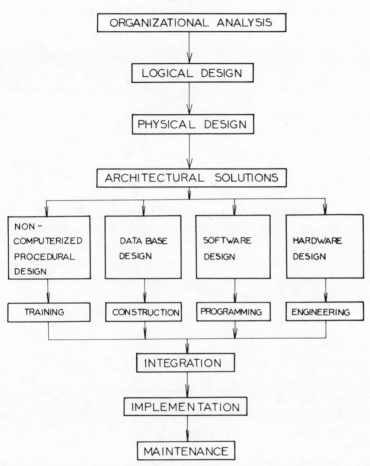

midi), the mini proper, the micromini. Figure 1.3 shows the perspectives for the 1980s, and the specific orientation of each of these markets.

Technologically, the evolution of the maxicomputer resembled the "big motor" approach with the main drive shaft which we had in factories at the beginning of the Industrial Revolution. The evolution of the mini can be considered as a data handling counterpart to that of small motors (fractional power): "one motor per tool," "one mini per office."

Three Levels of Sophistication

Figure 1.2 underscored the issue of noncomputerized procedures. Typically, such procedures either escaped the attention of the analyst because their user was

Figure 1.3
Introduction of minicomputers based on semiconductors

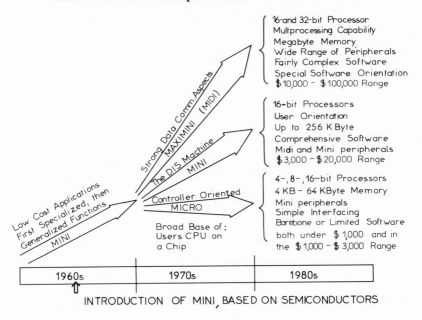

reluctant to identify them, or did not justify their handling by computer for cost/benefit reasons. DIS takes a totally new approach. We may now speak of the effective distribution of functions to be done locally. This definitely has an impact on computer design, input–output processors, front-end communications processors, intelligent terminals, etc., as a means of performing given functions. But the underlying issue is much broader than the functions referred to.

The salient problem in DIS design is the decision to use one of three levels of sophistication in projecting the new system.

The first level is *distributed processing* which is the implementation of one set of logical functions within multiple physical devices. Basically, it is the standalone minicomputer. The distribution of processing is realized through local or remote computers, with or without their own input–output devices and data base.

The second level of sophistication, which necessarily demands much more in terms of systems studies, is that of the *distributed data base*. It is one logical set of data stored at multiple physical locations interconnected and integrated among themselves. It is here that the avant-garde companies and financial institutions are working at the moment. For the next few years the main intellectual effort will center on this field, deciding which organizations will push ahead. The distribution of the data base poses many systems challenges, among them the definition of the "primary" files needed to tune the DB in the case of mutations and discrepancies.

The next, higher level of sophistication is the *distributed operating system* involving the distribution of DB processing and network control. This is the true distributed intelligence system. It embraces such features as downline loading, unattended operations, total network control, and other key features which will find their fulfillment in the 1980s. Current examples include Arpanet,* Telenet, Tymnet, Datapac, Transpac, and other networks with distributed data communications architecture and data base facilities. In the evolving symmetric or balanced networks, no single host is in total control of the system and all computers within the network can control their own processes. We shall return to this issue and treat it in detail.

Let us summarize these definitions. Distributed processing involves systems where large amounts of information are stored on media. But the data is *not* organized as a data base. This is the aim of distributed data bases. In turn, DDP† and DDB among themselves do not necessarily make a data communications system. This is the goal of distributed operating systems whose aim is to assure communications control while avoiding highly redundant storage.

At each level of sophistication, the designer must be aware that a basic reason for distributed intelligence is the impossibility of mastering extreme complexity. Large systems projects suffer problems different than those of small systems.

Other Dimensions of DIS

Three additional dimensions of distributed information systems are operations, management, and applications development. A basic factor here is the logical structure of the applications segments or functions to be performed. Are the tasks or functions mutually dependent, or are they independent from one another? Inventory management, personnel systems, manufacturing control, order entry, accounts receivable and payable may be either totally independent or interdependent to a greater or lesser degree. With maxicomputers most of these systems have been operated (with duplications, discrepancies, and incompatibilities) independently from one another because of the dual influence of the accounting machines era and the remoteness of the central installation.

But times are changing. The minicomputer brings the equipment capability near the user and with it the problems and responsibilities. Users are now responsible for entering their own data into the system correctly. They must watch the following:

1. Cost of accomplishing a desired processing or logical function·
2. Time needed to develop and implement the process
3. Maintenance requirements

*At present, New York's Citibank seems to be the first and only institution with a private and functioning Arpanet-like system.
    † "Distributed data processing" as distinguished from the classic DP, "data processing."

4. Controls and standards relating to the process
5. Utility or relative priority of a given function
6. Expected results
7. Risks associated with a decentralized, distributed approach

There is no central computer department to blame anymore and to complain about to top management.

However, DIS is not certain to be an outright success just because it is modern. The procedural and the logical studies hold the key to success or to failure, and with them the architectural project which we shall be discussing.

Division of Labor

The division of labor and the specialization of functions have become possible with distributed processing. The integration of these functions into a working ensemble comes about with the study and implementation of distributed data bases. Does distribution of processing mean no centralized standards with everyone getting a computer and doing as he wants? Definitely not. This would be chaos. But what is the "right" level of distributed functions? This is, indeed, very debatable.

Centralization and decentralization vary over time by broad function, by specific task, by topology and local problem. The same is true when you look at the means for implementing a distributed information system. Some companies just distribute the hardware, leaving all organizational studies, system analysis, and programming centralized. Others also decentralize some of the software development functions. Those who distribute everything, including the control, are rare.

No matter which policy is chosen, there is a need for coordination. This involves:

1. Planning the use of all resources—human capital and equipment—under one authority.
2. Communicating with users on current requirements and on projected requirements for the next one to three years.
3. Integrating the job of software analysts and programmers with the current requirements and within the longer range plan.
4. Projecting the system architecture for the development of network approaches (including host and terminal topology and usage).
5. Providing for "user exits" to help develop a creative effort at the periphery.
6. Projecting the use of packages to bring future requirements for software usage within a nearly 50–50 basis between packages and homemade programs.
7. Maintaining and updating the timetable for all the above-mentioned functions.
8. Initiating and administering design reviews.

Provided that these functions are carried out ably, centralization or decentralization becomes an option to be decided by management.

Figure 1.4

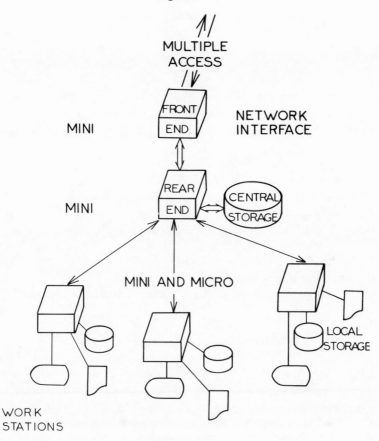

What must be done in DIS is to match the management organization, functions, and operating principle of the industry or financial institution contemplating a change from a centralized to a decentralized approach. However, for this to be done properly we must formulate a total DIS solution.

Let us take as an example the guiding principles followed by the Bank of America and Citibank. They may be stated in three main points:

1. Put the computer power into the hands of the decision maker.
2. Build the concept of the individual task, but keep in operation a central DB accessible to all.
3. Project a data communication network for system access and project it in a cost-effective manner.

Figure 1.4 exemplifies this approach. Work stations are installed at the branch-office level. Each work station is dedicated to a particular task or function. The

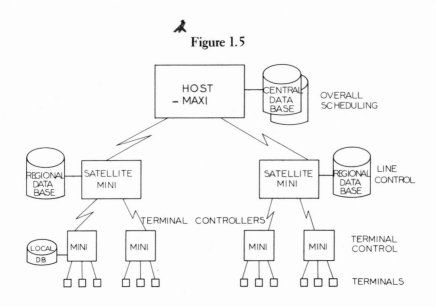

Figure 1.5

minicomputers and microcomputers in this network are linked in a hierarchical structure. But hierarchy does not necessarily mean a vertical organization.

Alternatives: Vertical and Horizontal

A distributed information system may be organized along centralized control* (asymmetric, vertical, hierarchical), decentralized control (symmetric, ring, horizontal), or hybrid lines. The choice depends on the system architecture to be adopted.

Figure 1.5 illustrates an asymmetric centralized control approach with a host processor, satellite processors (usually mini), terminal controllers, and near-by and remote terminals. This equipment is connected vertically and the whole system is controlled by the host processor. The *host* is an information processor which provides supporting services to users and/or other processors. The *satellite* is an information processor which communicates with and depends on a host for services and guidance.

One should not confuse a vertical or hierarchical control system with a hierarchical information system, which may be totally decentralized in terms of architecture and control.

Two or more processors operating in an "equal partner" relationship constitute a symmetric or horizontal system. For instance, three minicomputer centers may be maintained in different cities provided with links which allow them to communicate freely; see Figure 1.6. Jobs may be transferred between centers; data load may be leveled. The failure of one center will *not* affect the whole system. Each center may

---

*A centralized control solution which should not be confused with a "centralized system."

Figure 1.6

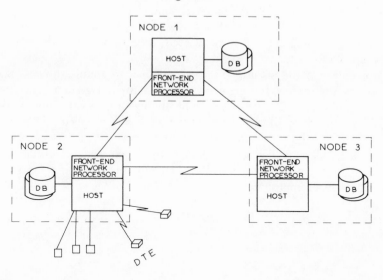

control one or more front ends, FE, and each front end one or more terminals. For their part, the front end and terminal controllers support data entry operations by providing the appropriate screen format for data input; assist in detecting errors and report them back to the terminal user for corrective action; send correct transactions to the host (whether horizontal or vertical); and help the host's data load by removing and handling locally a considerable amount of processing and data storage functions.

Thus, the distributed information system reflects logical relationships among functional jobs and physical relationships among components. Actual implementations may use a variety of physical communications network structures.

The data communications, DC, functions include polling and selecting or other discipline, the choice of lines, code translation, data verification and data blocking, band rates, and line disciplines. In the general case, the data communications work may be done effectively by distributed minicomputers or by maxicomputers with colossal memory-eating operating systems.

Conclusion

A distributed information system is *not* a decentralized system, as commonly spoken about. It is a hierarchical, structured, organized system with discipline and rules to be enforced at all times. Violation of these rules results in the negation of its advantages—and an eventual disintegration of the system.

In a hierarchical system, the rules have to do with security and protection, data accessibility, the use of shared resources, timeliness, accuracy, and economics.

Standards are also necessarily directed to the issues of transferability of programs between hosts, common data definitions, common operating procedures, and line of command or unity. Rules and standards applied within a DIS environment will help move processing close to the end users, improve response, decrease transit delays, and dwarf costs.

Not only can the small specialized components (minis, micros) perform functions cost effectively, but the benefits to be derived range from reliability and maintainability, to modularity, expandability throughput, response time, workplace terminal independence, low implementation cost, and simplicity in applications software.

Figure 1.7 identifies the factors entering a DIS design. Some constitute the basic background of the new informatics. Its actual authority is acquired from the very momentum of accomplishment.

Table 1.1

	1. DIS concept: processing, data base, operating system	2. New systems methodology	3. Microelectronics	4. Data terminal equipment: mini, micro, new terminals	5. Data communications equipment & communications lines; satellites & fibers	6. Protocols	7. Networking: routing and recovery	8. Systems architecture	9. Data base management	10. Security, privacy, encryption recovery	11. Interactive approach and user exits	12. Operating system support	13. Maintenance	14. Cost effectiveness
1. System planning														
2. Logical design														
3. Physical design														
4–5. Construction														
6–7. Test														
8. Installation														
9. Operation														
10. Maintenance														

2

Rising Markets and Falling Prices

As in the early 1950s, the 1980s present new horizons in terms of professional perspectives of systems development and of machine components. The most significant breakthrough yet has been the semiconductor technology: the data processing industry, including every factor from supplier activity to user costs, will account for 13 percent of the nation's gross national product by 1990. Further, some 20 percent of the total United States labor force will be required to have some knowledge of data processing; about 65 percent of that labor force will be dependent to some measure on the use of data processing. By 1990 there will be approximately 175,000 large-scale general-purpose computer sites in various parts of the United States, not including the close to 1,000,000 dedicated systems for such applications as process control, inventory management, and data entry.

World revenues for United States computer manufacturing firms were $26.6 billion at the end of 1976 and are expected to be $51 billion by the end of 1981. United States computer service firms' revenues were $5.3 billion at the end of 1976 and are projected to be $13 billion by 1981. United States computer equipment manufacturers dominate the world market, accounting for 87 percent of the world's computers by value. For 1990 it will be safe to multiply by a factor of nearly 4 the figures projected for 1981.

The business opportunities brought about by sharply falling prices have rarely been matched in the past. In fact, if we group together microelectronics, personal and home computers, optical fibers and satellite communications, since the beginning of the Industrial Revolution one can say that no other line of business has had such a growth potential: the railways in the mid-nineteenth century, the telephone from the late nineteenth century, the automobile from the beginning of this century, and, more particularly, the post-war years, the radio since its domestication in the mid-1920s, and the computer for the last quarter century.

The new market horizons which are now opening will take a good ten years before they are in full swing. In another decade or so they will reach maturity. Until nearly the end of the twentieth century, we shall see a time of transition. This is significant. Opportunity comes with uncertainty and as such it can mean wealth or bankruptcy, depending on the ability to overcome obstacles.

Uncertainty within a competitive business environment means that one has to keep many irons in the fire. These many irons—research, development, production*, marketing, maintenance service, and inventories—add up to prohibitive costs, unless we make, from the drafting board stage, a product which can grow and shrink at the same time, and by so doing exploit the mainlines, and even some of the darker corners of the market, to the fullest possible extent.

The markets created by modern technology have no time for monoliths. The fiercely competitive market in which we live does not permit us to rest on our laurels—we risk becoming obsolete or slipping out of business altogether. This is as true of products as it is of skills. Experimental evidence shows that the half-life of a technology-intense job performance, including the basic skills and education, is about five years. And the half-life of a technology-based product is generally shorter than that.

Inventory of Images

To appreciate the impact on our jobs and on our lives of the new technologies,† we should start with the fundamentals. First we have to focus on the right image.

A person's mental inventory of images largely determines his ability to understand events. The General Motors Corporation, for instance, would be quite inconceivable in ancient Greece because the people of that epoch did not possess the requisite set of images for industrial and commercial operations of that type and size. Columbus would never have set sail westward had he not had an image of the round world and a high value system for spices. The Industrial Revolution in England cannot be explained simply by the availability of coal and iron; it was much more determined by a change in basic images. Without the requisite images of simple things, more complex ones cannot be understood. Basic images are so important that the ideas or concepts necessary for progress will always precede the actual development.

If the requisite images do not exist, technological improvements that are made accidentally will not be accepted and imitated; in fact, they would even be suppressed. The importance of having the necessary images in "public inventory" before a new development can come into common use can hardly be underestimated. Market research tells us not so much whether or not a product or service will be accepted, but rather points out what necessary images of perceived value or functional importance are already in "inventory."

---

*The real competitive edge in microelectronics is not the discovery of the physical principle but *production technology*. Sixty years ago the same was true of lamps.

†This discussion is not intended to enter the technical details of the issue. Emphasis here is on the dynamics.

If important images are missing, then it is necessary to create them before the service will be commonly accepted. Pioneers in new services often find slow acceptance. This is precisely because they are in the new image-building business. The second and third entries into the marketplace benefit from the expensive image-building activities of the first. But the first has an important asset, if he knows how to use it. He has the opportunity to formulate the new service image and thus dictate the basis for new additional service options that can be added to the new service at a later time.

This is what is happening today with rising markets and falling prices. Since 1975 vast improvements in price/performance ratios have become commonplace. The trend is continuous. Since 1950 the cost per bit of information in high-speed storage has decreased 1,000-fold. In the past seven years the cost of computer memory was reduced at the rate of nearly 30 percent per year, that of discs dropped by about 40 percent and costs for computer logic declined by 25 percent per year. New innovations, hoped for yesterday and ordered today to be delivered tomorrow, have a high probability of being called obsolete before installation. Obsolete does not mean useless; rather, better, more cost-effective alternatives are steadily being made available. Such alternatives alter radically the information systems concepts and their implementation.

The Essence of Change

In the information systems profession change is the essence of our work as we strive for continuing productivity improvement as much in equipment as in people. The manager who cannot cope with change, plan for change, and produce continuing change will not be effective. This role is new and different from the traditional roles of management. Change brings to professionals both risk and opportunity, but definitely the greatest opportunity (and test) is in the marketplace.

If the automobile industry had progressed on the same curve as computers in the last twenty years, we would have been able to buy for under sixty dollars a medium-sized car and this price would have dropped to less than five dollars within five years. On the average, given computer power, prices have dropped by a factor of fifty during the last two decades as concerns system prices. But the decline is much more dramatic for some of the components. Memory prices declined by about 30 to 40 percent annually between 1971–77. And the extrapolated values indicate a cost per component by 1980–82 approaching $.001.

Three crucial variables characterize the "bit of information" in twenty-five years of development (1953–79):

Cost—the reduction has been 1,000:1

Volume—the ratio is 800:1

Speed—the most development of all with a ratio of 100,000:1

Cost reductions in computer technology were the result of:

1. Better fundamental understanding of the materials used
2. Development of computerized design techniques
3. Sophisticated manufacturing tools
4. New techniques used to package increasingly dense circuits
5. Volume production
6. The push of competition

Today, a minicomputer with 64-kilobytes can be bought for less than $10,000. It is projected that by 1982 advances in microelectronics will bring the cost of the 64-kilobyte chip to about $10.

If economies in energy consumption had kept pace with other economies, such as the increase in disc drive capacity, the acute energy problems we are faced with today would have been solved long ago. Disc drive capacity jumped from 5 megabytes in the early 1960s to over 500 megabytes today. Price per megabyte has decreased nearly a hundredfold during this same period. Costs of hand-held calculators have declined a hundredfold in ten years.

Technology is the engine of social, economic, and industrial change. The "Willies Ware" rule aptly states that when something changes by a factor of 10, fundamental new effects will be presented, and management decisions will change. Such changes will be reflected in every walk of industrial and business life in terms of costs, speed, and facilities.

The Speed of Change

A measure of the speed of change is illustrated by the giant jumps in computing circuitry. In the 1940s things happened in computers at the rate of 1 per second. Switching in the human nervous system is about 10^2 per second. By now even minicomputers work at 10^6 per second. Before too long this performance will be topped by 10^2; things will be happening within the computer at 10^8 per second. So, in 30 years switching speed in computer technology advanced by 10^8 and exceeded the best of natural information systems by one million times.

Progress would necessarily retreat without the powerful computer systems and data communications networks upon which a service-oriented society depends. The criteria for future choices will reflect values different from those we know today: precision, timeliness, and basic economies will become facts. Paper will become the exceptional medium for human communications, being replaced by on-line storage and retrieval devices with soft-copy alternatives. Computer networks will bring the information faculty to every workplace.

Throughout the coming decade, and in the 1990s, every time we take a step we shall find that, within the short span of two to four years the cost of new technology approaches the cost of the old technology but at a much higher capacity. The 4-kilobit (KB) chip today sells at $3 to $4 OEM.* This will be the price of the 64-

*Original equipment manufacturer.

Figure 2.1

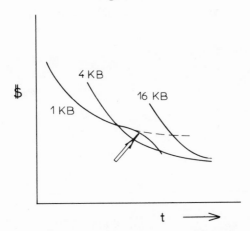

kilobit chip in a couple of years and eventually of the 128-kilobit chip. Figure 2.1 demonstrates that when the 4-kilobit chip became cheaper than the 1 kilobit, the latter dropped dramatically in price. Such is the rule of swift technology: A product which is overtaken by developments *must* leave the "normal" curve and sell at a dramatically lower cost—or nobody will buy it anymore.

Notice that such developments result from a sharply advancing production methodology on the same family of physical principles. If the basic technology changes, then things may move even faster. In seven or eight years we should expect 10,000 times greater performance from Josephson (tunnel junction) technology; a megabyte storage chip may cost approximately $30 by then. The whole systems profession will be affected by this.

A 100- to 500-fold improvement in performance, over current levels, if practical by 1985, will be sufficient to change our style of programming. Even with the now classic lines of rapid evolution, without the effects of the Josephson technology, it is projected that *by 1982 1 megabyte of high-speed memory will cost the equivalent of 1 man-month of programming.*

A further 500-fold increase in speeds and capacities will dramatically alter the way we program future computers. There will no longer be much concern about efficient code or wasteful use of main memory. Working on-line, programmers and analysts will be able to try all possible solutions to a problem since it would take only a few nanoseconds per try. Trial and error, interactive analysis, and programming analysis would drastically change the way we create software. Cost considerations will be radically altered. Today it costs five times the price of a minicomputer to do the analysis and programming for just one shift per day. With the 500-fold increase in speed, one hour of computer time may take a million and a half man-hours to program. New ways have to be found and the impact of chip technology on certain traditional, mechanical tasks may be felt before too long. For the programmer the problems of constructing and verifying software should be met at the chip level. On-

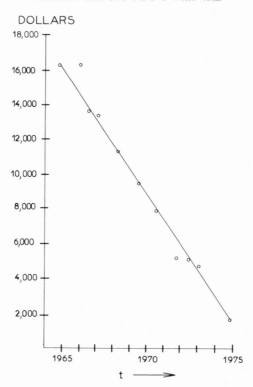

Figure 2.2
Medium cost of a PDP-8 with 4KB

line analysis, on-line programming, even specialized analysis and programming computers, which are rarities today, may become commonplace tomorrow.

In considering computer-aided analysis and programming, we should not forget that although the computer industry has been incredibly successful at expanding equipment capabilities while reducing costs and package size, there is still quite a way left to go before the ultramicrocomputer or picocomputer becomes a reality. Picocomputers will find their way in a full gamut of audio-visual materials and workbooks, instructor-led and laboratory sessions, and on-line or standalone terminals to serve professionals and for the training of a vast population of users in an equally immense aray of possibilities.

Market Characteristics

Abundant marketing documentation states that the most striking characteristic of the microelectronics industry has been a persistent and *rapid decline in the cost of a* *given electronic function.* It is now possible to put the computing power* of a computer that cost $1 million in the early 1950s on a chip that costs $20 to $30. That same chip cost $100 in 1978.

Much of this cost reduction has come from remarkable technological break-throughs in semiconductor processing. Minicomputers originally evolved as small processors that conceptually were almost like components. They were usually part of a larger, more complex system. Now, users have become so sophisticated, and the minicomputers so powerful and flexible, that the same machine can be used both as a component of one system and as complete standalone equipment. Prices have also fallen as a result of this product flexibility—its ability to hit more than one market, and to do so successfully. This is the case of the PDP-8 which more than any other machine helped Digital Equipment Corporation (DEC) on its way to becoming a billion-dollar corporation. Figure 2.2 illustrates the success of this story.

Another portion of the rapid decline in cost can be accounted for in terms of a learning curve: the more experience an industry has the more efficient it becomes. Table 2.1 presents ten years of price structure of the Hewlett-Packard product line.

However, as manufacturers know so well, and users are starting to appreciate, computer products are elusive when the total cost is considered. The PDP-11, introduced in 1970, has cost its manufacturer in hardware and software investment an estimated $1 billion—with the lion's share on the software side. Being a highly successful computer, it has given its manufacturer many billions of dollars in return. Such investments are justified because of the size of the market. In the United States alone the market for minicomputers grows by some 30 to 40 percent per year. The market for business application of minicomputers grows by 50 to 60 percent per year. The United States accounts for 50 percent of the world market, with Western Europe accounting for the other 30 percent.

Minicomputers and microcomputers are predicted to reach a cumulative market of $30 billion by 1985, while the minicomputer peripherals market may total $37 to $40 billion. Figures 2.3 and 2.4 give, respectively, in value and in numbers (per year) computer and minicomputer trends. More than $1 billion in minicomputer equipment was shipped to United States in 1976, bringing major changes in how an estimated 175,000 installations manage the economic and organizational aspects of information processing.

There are some 200 independent companies which currently produce mini-peripherals in addition to the minicomputer mainframers themselves. The way things look, software and peripherals have become the most profitable portions of a minicomputer system. It is also foreseen that enough minicomputers will be purchased over the next few years to provide economies of scale in software development.

During the next decade, the largest dollar hardware sales will be in alpha-numeric display terminals, printers, and magnetic discs. The alphanumeric display terminal's large sales are due to its use as a major on-line data entry unit which replaces batch processing with transaction type processing. The floppy disc and the

*But *not* the peripherals' power.

Table 2.1

The Pricing of a Product Line (prices in $1,000)

Systems	1968	1973	1974	1975	1976	1977	1979 Higher speed	1979 Lower cost
1,000	70					36 (with 15 megabyte disc)	31	22
2,000	100 (with 1.5 megabyte)					62 (with 15 megabyte disc; 128 kilobyte memory)	discontinued	
3,000		130 (with 5 megabyte disc)	4	2	1.5	110 (with 50 megabyte disc; 128 kilobyte memory)	94 (with 50 megabyte disc; 256 kilobyte memory)	62 (with 50 megabyte disc; 256 kilobyte memory)
Complete 8 KWords with circuits		10	4	2	1.5	0.75	discontinued	
CPU		24 (with 8 KWords)	2.6	2.6	1	6.5 (with 8 kilobyte) 14 (with 128 kilobyte)	2.8 (with 128 kilobyte; 650 nanoseconds access)	3.5 (with 128 kilobyte; 350 nanoseconds access)
Disc cost per 1 megabyte		25	2.6	2.6	1	0.28		

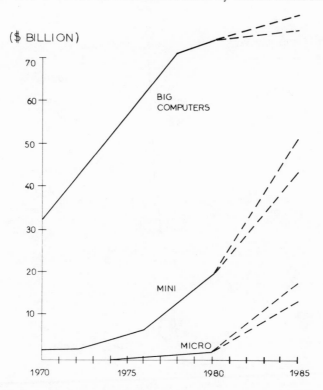

Figure 2.3
Total value of worldwide installations made by United States firms

($ BILLION)

BIG
COMPUTERS

MINI

MICRO

1970   1975   1980   1985

one-million byte mini disc have opened computerization to the small businessman and will see a great increase in annual sales.

With the trend toward multiple terminals, the number of units sold by 1985–86 may jump to 2.8 billion units, compared with 150,000 units valued at $150 million in 1976. Not surprisingly, competition among the minicomputer manufacturers, independent peripherals companies, and software houses is extremely fierce. All three groups project to supply the market with complete turnkey systems.

The Communications Impact

Well-run industries reduce their costs (in constant dollars) by 20 to 30 percent each time their cumulative output doubles. Examining data for the semiconductor industry, we find that integrated circuit costs have declined by 28 percent with each doubling of the industry's experience. But where do the communications costs stand?

Figure 2.4
Number of installations in the world

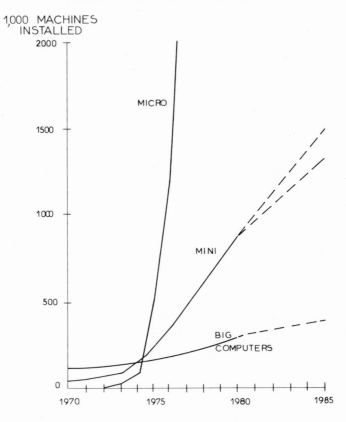

1,000 MACHINES
INSTALLED

The answer is that as of today, price reductions in the broad area of communications lag behind. Worldwide, the industry is too regulated, too rigid, does not face enough competition, and though many breakthroughs in physics come from telephone laboratories (the transistor story at AT&T being an example), not enough was done during the 1950s and the 1960s to move ahead in cost effectiveness. As a result, it is not surprising that price cuts in communications lag far behind a comparable feat in computers. AT&T for instance, stated in paid advertisements that between 1966 and 1975 the cost of telephone communications increased 4 percent, while during the same period of time the cost of living jumped by 74 percent. In steady dollars this makes a 40 percent reduction in price in ten years or less than 4 percent per year—which is a small fraction of what the computer industry has given its clientele over the same period of time.

Here are some interesting statistics on how much voice communications cost around the world. They show how many hours a person living in each country must work to pay for his basic telephone service for one year:

United States	26 hours
Switzerland	35 hours
United Kingdom	76 hours
Austria	104 hours
Japan	175 hours
France	179 hours

There is a definite gap between the benefits gained by technology and what the consumer receives in return.

While the cost of personnel has increased (at least in the United States) an estimated 4 to 6 percent per year in real terms, it is also true that due to technology, manufacturing costs have fallen 80 percent in this decade. In different terms, manufacturing costs drop much faster than prices, and lower prices—if effected—call forth more customers and a wider market.

Telephone people would answer that their industry is capital hungry (and so is the computer's because of the rental policy), or that the telephone has not yet shown the growth of the computer's market (yet the telephone market doubled during the last three years, at least in some European countries). Telephone people may also point out, and with reason, that the annual usage of logic gates or bits of memory has increased 2,000 times in 17 years. In 1960 approximately 500 million transistors were produced. By 1977 an estimated 1 trillion equivalent functions or bits were manufactured and shipped. But such an argument forgets that the telephone industry, just like the computer industry, is one of the big users of these gates.

Systemwise, the most significant advance in communications is in the data communications field with value-added networks, store and forward, packet switching, and the international standards which are now evolving.

The new rallying cry in the data communications world is X.25. Ever since it became a standard this higher level communications protocol for linking computers and terminals to packet networks has drummed up support around the world. In the line component, too, developments during the coming years will be exciting. The four most significant are satellite communications, optical fibers, digital communications, and dedicated microprocessors for each line. These developments backed by able management operating within a competitive market are expected to revolutionize communications.

By the early to mid-1980s when communication satellites will master long distance traffic, teleprocessing costs may drop to between 1/40 and 1/50 of those prevailing today. And it is said that if AT&T could replace the copper in twisted pair and in coaxial cables with optical fibers, then recover and sell the copper to the market, it could pay with the proceeds all the costs of manufacturing, laying, and servicing the optical fibers. The result would be a 25 to 30 times higher transmission rate at no extra cost.

The significant advantages of fiber optics in computers and communications are wideband width in the microwave range, electronic isolation and no interference, and loss of only two decibels per kilometer. These represent better integrity than that characterizing microwave techniques.

Developments in microprocessors and digital telecommunications will not only have an impact on the telephone industry and related sectors, but such developments foretell a future in which personal computing is a widespread reality.

Service Fallouts

The earliest computers utilized discrete components consisting of individual transistors, resistors, and capacitors. As components became more complex, technology advanced so that components could be integrated on a chip.

Most early minicomputers utilized small-scale and medium-scale integration with up to 100 functions on a board. In 1970 a 16-bit minicomputer central processing unit consisted of ten printed circuit boards containing more than 500 integrated packages with about 1,800 gates and 200 flip-flops. By 1975 there were only one or two printed circuit boards per machine with about 100 packages, 2,000 gates, and 250 flip-flops. By the 1980s it may be possible to have 200,000 transistors per chip or roughly ten times the current level of complexity.

Let us keep track of these changes, for their aftermaths will be long range. Self-maintenance, assisted by on-line diagnostics, in one of the best fallouts. This is the dream of the weary user waiting for field service which may now become a reality. Another major impact of cheap circuitry is on the location of computer power. It becomes more and more feasible to distribute computer power to the points where information originates or is needed instead of transmitting all data to and from a central computer installation. Distributed information systems, regardless of the definition used, serves as a focal point around which users can bring the latest technology into the organization and, by the same token, reduce their operational costs.

New technology is very important, not because of scientific excitement—no matter how great this may be—but as a function of the economic considerations as they impact the end-user. Manufacturers must have a product that fulfills requirements at a fair price so that they make a profit and the buyer is happy. When the end-user buys a product, he doesn't want to get one which is at the end of its life, or one which is just starting and has many failures. He aims to keep ahead of time; to get a service out of the product which is able to grow and develop; and to have, somehow, a company relation with the supplier: Is the supplier committed to him? To the market? Does it inderstand his problem? Will it support the product it sells to him?

The new products will be those made by people who understood and assimilated all their predecessors' successes, who are in complete possession of the techniques of their time, and have a full awareness of what makes the customer tick.

3

Three Generations of Networks

The functions, capabilities, and possible implications of data communications systems can be better appreciated by taking a brief look at the origins of computer technology.

The era of the commercially available data processor, as we know it today, started with Univac 1 and the IBM series 701, 702, 650. At the time, both appealed primarily to the batch processing business machines market, and for good reason. In 1952–53 IBM and Remington Rand (in that order) controlled the punched card, accounting machines, and related equipment market.* An accounting machine of the IBM 401 type had no teletransmission problems to cope with. It simply didn't possess the facility which brings the data communications problem into perspective. This is equally true of the highly successful IBM 650 in the 1950s which employed the 401 as a basic unit for input–output.

Both Univac and IBM integrated the computer with the accounting machines product line and sold the advancement in data handling presented by computer technology† as an extension of old concepts, but not as something totally new. The early users maintained an outlook fairly similar to that of the vendors. The story of computers might have been totally different had the first machines been launched by AT&T or GTE. This situation prevailed in the early and mid-1950s in terms of applications, since in its early configuration the computer answered three needs: arithmetic calculation, logical operations, and internal storage (though limited by the fact that the early media were bulky and, correspondingly, of low storage capacity).

*Though equipment was also used, particularly during World War II, for scientific calculations, this was, firstly, a rather exceptional use and, secondly, the card programmed approaches adopted for mathematical formulas were of a totally different concept than computers as we know them today.

†Particularly the stored program capabilities (ill-appreciated at the time except by geniuses like Von Neumann and Oppenheimer) and the memory capacity of the machine.

The Early Periods

Historically, the development of computers is comprised of three periods. During the *first period*, about 1950–1957, the central processors disposed of input–output routines limited to the communication of data via classic peripheral units which were largely batch oriented.

In the 1950s we spoke of "input-bound" and of "output-bound" operations. The problem of early users was to identify and then obtain the necessary media which would eliminate bottlenecks at both the input and output ends of the system. This state of affairs is germane to the hardware components. In terms of software, it was not until 1958 that the first input–output control system (IOCS) routines start being used; at about the same time the first experience in long-distance data communications took place: a tape to tape data transmission between the Andrews Air Force Base in the United States and the SHAPE Headquarters near Orleans, France.

This experience opened the way to the *second period* characterized by the input–output control of peripheral units, by means of specially written software, and the first batch-type data communication.

Although in a way these two developments are distinct from one another, they produced a joint effect: the beginning of the *third period*, whose particularity was the development and use of special software necessary to drive terminals at long distance and, along with them, the needed interfaces with the telephone line.

This experience had nothing in common with the control of a communications network as we know it today. The terminals were extremely simple, indeed, just typewriters with a line controller. Yet, the availability of simple, unsophisticated terminals and some basic software induced imaginative minds to play with a new idea: time sharing.

Time sharing is a milestone in data communications. By 1963–64 there was evidence that users might be amenable to abandoning the old habit of batch processing; they considered sharing the facilities provided by a centrally located machine. The possibility of handling on-line data processing problems was, here and there, taking root.

The asynchronous mode had its day. But users (who quite often, if incorrectly, tried batch solutions through time-sharing terminals)* established through practice the need for more efficient alternatives. It took a few more years until finally synchronous protocols were accepted.

Point-to-Point

Point-to-point data transmission was the usual solution for these operations. Transmission was character by character, and a message was composed of as many characters as necessary. But overhead expenses also boomed as data communica-

---

*Time sharing, correctly implemented, simply means rapid access to a small amount of information. It is the negation of batch. However, many users misapply time sharing as on-line batch capability.

tions loads increased. Cost brought the need for efficiency, and this concern, coupled with the advances made in technology, led to the *fourth period* (mid to late 1960s) in computer development characterized by the advancement of synchronous protocols and the more sophisticated teleprocessing software, specific, however, to the type of terminal.

The *lack of standardization*, which characterized this period, is with us even today. As data loads boomed, gaping holes in data communications came to light. As usual, necessity spurred new research. In 1967 IBM introduced the binary synchronous communication, BSC, protocols. Synchronous communications were already demonstrating a definite advantage over asynchronous by effectively using resources.

Parallel to the developments in systems which characterized the late fifties and the decade of the sixties, we experienced an evolution in data communications equipment. One is tempted to classify the tape-to-tape devices used for batch transmission as the "beginning." As regards terminals, this "beginning" includes the largely unintelligent units transmitting in an asynchronous mode (lates 1950s, mid-1960s).

Let us recall that early computers integrated punched card and accounting machines as their input–output media. The first consoles were rudimentary; the terminals were teletypewriters and teletypes. There was no data communications industry as such. By the late sixties the situation had changed. The impact of terminals manufacturers started being felt, and the mainframe companies launched terminal product lines. Indeed, some of them, for instance, Univac, even set up a separate division.

The real-time applications of the mid-1960s (airline reservation systems, for example) gave impetus to the direction which the design of terminals should take. Video scopes came into perspective, and the term "soft copy" as opposed to "hard copy" started to be used.

The new terminals had many advantages over their predecessors. They used synchronous protocols, had buffers, and, applicationswise, became integrated into well-designed, though elementary, networks. Experiments were made with new approaches to telecommunication software, although the latter was largely machine dependent.

The First Generation

Data communications as a discipline, born with the ARPA Project, was to become one of the most dynamic fields in information technology. Earlier solutions were rudimentary by today's standards. They were private networks using the concepts of the fourth period (hence, asymmetric): centralized, starlike, with point-to-point and multidrop lines. Public networks started as an outgrowth of the private. Still, private networks are in the majority today, although inefficient as concerns the use of equipment, lines, and manpower. Economies of scale have not yet been realized

Figure 3.1

Network architecture of the first generation: Arpanet, Tymnet, and Cyclades

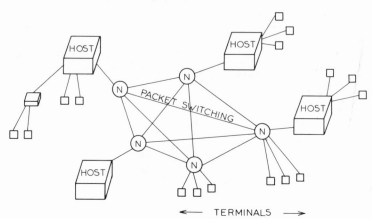

through the use of the private networks, and, generally speaking, it is doubtful if they will be. (Incidentally, by 1973 public networks had already started to develop.)

The faculties of a data communications network as we conceive it now were not present ten years ago. That is why a distinction between "period" and "generation" is necessary to keep up with established practices. The word *generation* has been consistently used in literature to identify hardware developments. *Period*, as used in this text, is related to the evolution of the systems concepts which often precede (though also sometimes follow) the hardware generation.

In the late sixties, when ARPA investigated packet-switching networks,* the need for a more efficient means than BSC was just starting to be felt. The image wasn't there, and the components of the data transmission systems were costly or limited in their capabilities. Memory was still expensive, which created the need to minimize buffers. The Node (minicomputer) could only handle up to three hosts, and, furthermore, had to be located near them; layout and organization were such as to render them not as reliable as desired. The network had to be very tight; besides, there wasn't enough traffic with which to load the network. The early concepts of the first generation were shaped by machine capability—and this dictated "what could be done."

Figure 3.1 gives a glimpse of the network architecture of the First Generation. Note the clear distinction between node† and host. Arpanet and Tymnet (both United States) and Cyclades (France) are examples.

---

*A communications network which employs "packets" as the basic unit of text transmission. A "packet" is a bit string of determined maximum length which is transmitted as a whole.

†Communication equipment placed at sensitive communication spots (nodes) to which bit strings can be directed via communications facilities using a unique destination address.

VAN
Figure 3.2
Switch to public data network concept

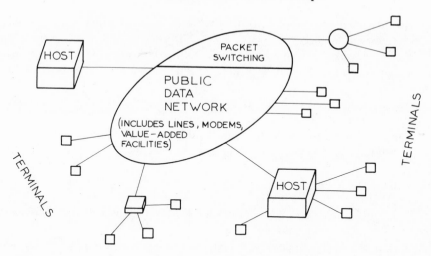

The Second Generation

With the first generation, machine capacity (host, node—individually), not cumulative network capacity, dictated what could be done. But the *fifth period* of conceptual development which started in the early seventies clearly demonstrated the need for software-controlled data transmission.* Furthermore, at the private network sites, though still behind Arpanet, users started to take an active hand in selecting the characteristics of the equipment they would employ, including the choice of components, microprocessors, memories, etc., with which they would build their own concentrators.

At the systems level, front ends started to become a favored solution. Performance made the difference—and people became aware of it.

Over a period of a few years, new types of hardware enhanced the principles which guided this fifth period. The dramatic drop in costs per bit of data storage, though just starting, opened new horizons. Memory capability was added at the terminal level.

As users became aware of a publicly offered network service, they appreciated that they could one day literally plug into a value-added carrier.† This concept, shown in Figure 3.2, is at the origin of the second generation.

---

*Typically stored at the host facility, the front ends, and the concentrator, rather than the value-added network (VAN) and the terminal itself which will characterize subsequent periods.

†Used synonymously with VAN. A communications network which employs common carrier facilities for transmission and provides in addition such services as path selection (routing), error detection, store and forward, retransmission, recovery, and so on.

Several differences between the first and the second generations of data communication networks should be noted:

All first generation networks (with the exception of Tymnet which is private) were government financed.

Public networks,* whether run by the telephone utility or by other commercial firms, came as an outgrowth of private networks. Economies of scale were the objectives.

The second generation benefited from the basic economics. The cost of buffer space was in the meantime reduced by a factor of 10.

➥ Nodes of the second generation can stand alone; see Figure 3.3.

Reliability in the second generation is considerably higher; 99.99 percent is the goal.

Duplex technology is used and the circuits can be highly loaded and quite efficiently at that.

The "hub" principle in data transmission has been adopted. Hub costs money, but results in better utilization of the lines.

Improvements in standards and performance are bringing data transmission costs down by factor 10.

The second generation offers store and forward facilities, and the user may attach both hosts and terminals at his discretion.

Typically, second generation networks observe the standard X.25. This is the mark of the times. Conceived in the early seventies, after the Arpanet experiences started coming into the public domain, and implemented in 1976–77, the second generation networks—Telenet (United States; commercial), Datapac (Canada; telephone utility) and Transpac (France; PTT†) were able to implement the new standards.

Merging Technologies

Among the new technologies is the virtual circuit idea. This is a point-to-point switched circuit over which data and commands (reset, interrupt, flow control) are transmitted. Virtual circuits may or may not, be a direct piece of wire, but are nevertheless a physical unit. The public network provides the routing and the flow control, giving the user a virtual circuit whenever he needs to communicate with another user. DIS implementation is thus enhanced.

Value-added networks, VAN, offer a multiple connection host interface; see Figure 3.4. This makes the private lines which came into existence with the centralized real-time approaches of the mid-1960s both very costly and obsolete. The economic trend which brought us from message to package switching has not

---

*Not to be confused with COAM—company owned and operated data networks.
†Poste, Telegraph, Telephone

Figure 3.3
Network architecture of the second generation: Telenet, Datapac, and Transpac

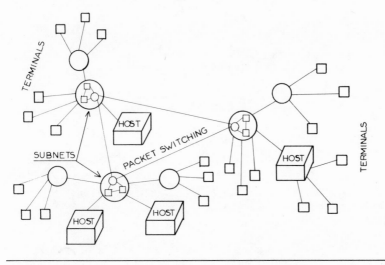

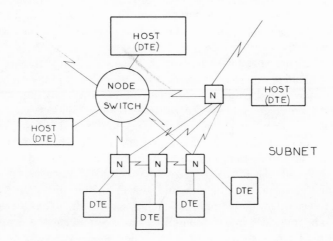

stopped. We are faced today with companies which are still living in the sixties with their centralized real-time solutions (while paying very dearly for them) while others have already moved into the eighties with DIS and VAN. The distributed information system thus has its roots in dollars, cents, and efficiency. By bringing data entry, computing, and storage to the point in the organization where the action takes place, distributed data systems have a much greater impact on information processing and on the architecture of the data system.

To summarize, the early to mid-1970s saw a fantastic expansion in private

Figure 3.4
Multiple connection host interface

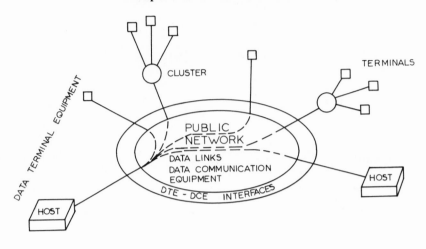

communication networks. The special software by type of terminal (or concentrator) became commonplace, while users started questioning the wisdom of emulating (usually IBM's line) communications software by type of device. To a very large extent, this was followed by small manufacturers who wanted to carve a share out of IBM's huge market.

Yet, no matter what the origins may be, this emulation of hardware opened new horizons and along with them the *sixth period* which, with minor exceptions began in the mid-1970s and is still gaining momentum. This is the time of distributed intelligence served by value-added carriers (Tymnet, Telenet, etc.) rather than through the private telephone lines of the third, fourth, and fifth periods. Beyond a doubt, the future telecommunication networks for data handling will be value-added: carriers with improved capabilities for error detection and correction, store and forward, and related data services.

Parallel to network structures and system architectures, users want, and manufacturers are on the point of producing, new hardware and software characteristics to be imbedded into the communications equipment now being projected. Typically, such terminals will incorporate a microprocessor, be very intelligent, and integrate in a telephone network, which follows the protocol X.25. The transition will take some years to settle down, and even in the late eighties there may be asynchronous terminals still in operation.* (Until the early sixties, IBM derived more income from punched card equipment than from computers). This, however, does not diminish the importance of being in the foreground of technology, to learn from the cost effectiveness of technological advancement. The producers of data systems should only be satisfied with leadership. The users should miss no opportunity to gain from the new horizons which technology is opening up.

*Indeed, today the asynchronous terminals form the majority.

Figure 3.5

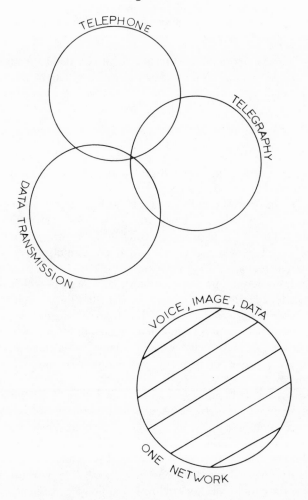

The merging of telephone (voice), telegraphy, telex, and data transmission into one single network (Figure 3.5) providing data, image, and voice facilities will have a colossal impact on the evolution of communications. It will bring about increased reliability, speeded up services, and drastic reductions in costs. This transition will present challenges both at the manufacturers' and at the users' sites. Telegraphy is a redundant process and is not even very reliable. Data transmission must be correct; it is better not to receive a message than to receive an erroneous one. On the other hand, data transmission is ten times more efficient than voice communications.

The merging communications technologies will open up tremendous capabilities:

1. *Teleconferencing* ("communicate—don't commute")

2. *Optimization of resources* (Use computers globally. When it is 7:00 P.M. in London, it is 10:00 A.M. in Los Angeles.)
3. *Serving the man with the problem (bringing the equipment capabilities to him, and not vice versa)*

It is obviously far more efficient to have common development and maintenance of the general-purpose communications facilities than to still have artificial (and obsolete) subdivisions because of the way systems have somehow developed.

Network Interfaces

We spoke earlier of coupling of intelligent terminals directly with value-added networks. This will have significant consequences for both users and manufacturers. The "pulling" of the network intelligence back into the terminal will open a new era of applications: remote batch, order entry, and point-of-sales credit verification. These are but a few of the possibilities which exist. Home computers will help optimize the use of lines (data, voice), and microcomputers will manage each distinct operation, including the lines themselves.

At the network level, VAN will take over many faculties which normally the individual user today must personally watch. Whether they are private or public, emphasis is on the words *value added*. This comprises functions such as monitoring, routing, journaling, error detection and correction. Such functions are a must in telecommunications. If the network does not provide them (and at present it does not), then we, the users—albeit in a more elementary way—must see them through and at a higher cost.

Monitoring is vital. It can be achieved both through hardware and software, distributed throughout the network. Actual monitoring is usually accomplished from one or a few control centers. By intelligent use of automatic remote checkout logic, including remote sensing of component failure, degradation,* and out-of-service conditions, failures may be detected and personnel dispatched for either node or channel repair. Statistics may be generated to measure the internal performance of the communications network, for instance, queue lengths, message sizes, line loads, time-up, overall response and routing, to aid in tuning the system and providing fault detection and correction. Many of these functions have been developed with the presently operating VAN. Others are currently under study.

Naturally, lessons learned from the first generation were applied both in the second and in the third, and although the basic concepts have changed, first generation networks are still going strong. Tymnet is a successful commercial operation which, among other firsts, has to its credit the concept of on-line maintenance; Arpanet helped build the very fine community of data communications scientists which exists today.

But the first generation also plays the vital role of the test bed on which some of the most advanced concepts are developed. One of these concepts is the integration of synchronous and asynchronous transmission together with packet switching for

---

*Gradual deterioration in performance.

Figure 3.6

Basic modes of host–terminal access. Packet BSC and asynchronous DTE are accepted. Network transmission is X.25.

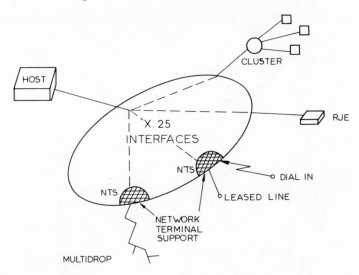

the reasons discussed in the preceding pages. The economies of synchronous transmission are basically the same as those of asynchronous but protocol conversion and local cost of communications are primary factors in making the choice.

It is so much better to have VAN facilities to which we can admit asynchronous, synchronous, and packet switching disciplines by providing the right ports for each; see Figure 3.6. Interfaces can be assured. The problem of polling is solved by hub polling and contention. Dial-in capabilities and automatic calling by terminals with significant local memory will open new horizons at the user's site.

All this is more than just distributed information systems. The high-speed memory, and quite likely the auxiliary memory as well, may no longer reside with concentrators, but with the terminal. The terminal will, in essence, be a minicomputer or microcomputer. The successors to Intel's 8080 will offer large-scale integration arithmetic, logical, and control functions on a chip. SDLC/HDLC will be on a chip and likewise the X.25 protocol. By the early eighties the 64-kilobit chip may well be commonplace. Terminals will necessarily be designed to support the network functions, augmenting the user's data communication abilities. The telephone set could be a microcomputer, and it will become difficult to distinguish a telephone set from a terminal.

On a macroscopic level, internetworking disciplines must be developed which will permit users of one network to communicate with those of another. Simultaneous multiple connections are needed and a new standard is being developed, the X.75, which will permit internetworking.

Figure 3.7
Network architecture of the third generation

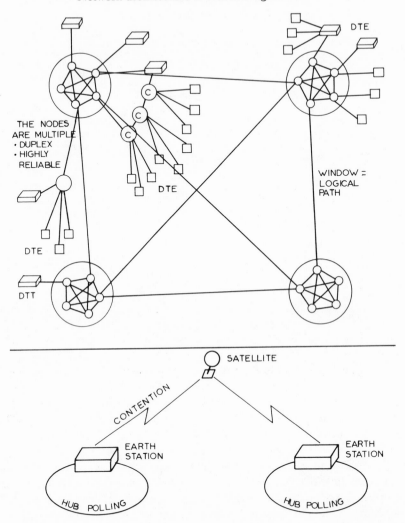

The Third Generation

The concepts which will characterize the third generation of data communication networks (Figure 3.7) are already being developed today.

Satellite communications will play a vital role.
Distance will play only a secondary role, or none at all.
Contention will be the prevailing discipline.

Figure 3.8
Solution to the problem of rigidity

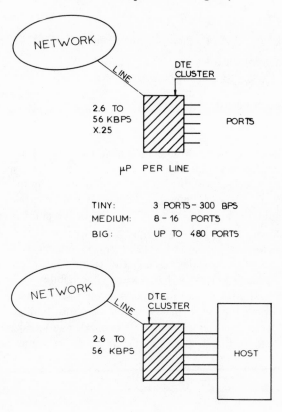

The network will keep track of the "windows" (logical paths; availability to receive) of the data terminal equipment, DTE, which it serves.

The DTE will have ample buffers.

Transmission lines will be characterized by high reliability.

Each line will have its own microprocessor and memory.

Communications systems will be highly modular: start small, then add new nodes and clusters.

Nodes and clusters will be of a different architecture in different parts of the network.

The user's DTE will specialize according to type and level of requirements.

Such networks will be designed over a number of years and will operate for long periods of time. They will be flexible and cost effective. The need for repair and maintenance will be studied from the beginning—at the drafting board. The same is true of the forecast of operations and of workability.

What are the most important factors for an optimum design?

Start with objectives.

Choose the transmission facilities.

Establish the switching methods.

Choose the topological layout.

Select the DTE equipment.

Settle on the protocols.

Establish the interfacing.

Selecting the DTE means to choose from alternatives. DTE clusters will be commonplace and connected to the network through intelligent lines of 2.6 to 56 working kilobits per second with the X.25 protocol or its successor. The DTE cluster will have a microprocessor which will probably come in three sizes: tiny—3 ports, 300 bits per second; medium—8–16 ports; big—up to 480 ports. A DTE cluster can serve a host through multiple lines (Figure 3.8) which is a good solution to the rigidity problem: modularity applied to the network's interface.

Organizational issues linking together the factory, the sales offices, and the headquarters, financial criteria (cost effectiveness), reliability and maintainability, and growth potential all will play an important role in structural decisions.

The user will need to define precisely what he wants, both for his own people and for the value-added carrier who will serve him. He cannot ask for "everything at the same time" as he did in the past, or, at least, he cannot afford to do so financially.

4

Backbone Operations

Network topology information is necessary for the nodes of a distributed computer and a communications network to communicate. Furthermore, since nodes and links sometimes crash, a scheme is needed to update this information.

The pivot point, and at the same time one of the major constraints in providing and upkeeping topology information, is the protocol. A topology information protocol must be quite general and remain unaffected as new nodes (hosts and switches) are implemented on the computer network.

Topologies can vary in their basic characteristics, depending, among other factors, on the area which they cover. As Table 4.1 demonstrates, we can distinguish among wide area, limited area, and internal computer structure. The latter will increasingly resemble a data communications network.

A different way of presenting this three-way classification is to distinguish among the following:

Remote Computer Networking	Local Networking	Multiprocessing
Aloha	Ethenet	Illiac, etc.
ARPANET	Spider (Bell Labs)	

Area-oriented classifications became important as computer communications grew from earlier implementations barely distinct from one another: real time RT, time sharing TS, telecommunications, and multiprocessing. Multiprocessing led to networking. Networks allow distributed multiprocessing.

Experience has demonstrated that substantial remodeling is necessary to achieve reliability, availability, modularity, and a reasonable compromise between good throughput, low delay, and good quality service as the network becomes increasingly complex.

Table 4.1

The network concept must be seen at three levels:

1. WIDE AREA

    Say, 100 to over 5,000 kilometers, characterized by

    Multiplicity of data communications media

    Synchronization

    Repeater problems

    Lack of direct control

2. LIMITED AREA

    Say, 500 to over 7,000 kilometers; typically

    Factory

    Office building

    Apartment building

3. INTERNAL COMPUTER STRUCTURE

Topological Description

Let us begin by looking back at the fundamentals. A typical computer and communications network is a collection of host computers connected by a communication subnetwork. This is a constellation of minicomputers (the switching nodes of the network) interconnected by bi-directional links (usually telephone lines).

A topological description of a network specifies the nodes and the links. But a general description, though necessary, is not sufficient. The other pillar is the procedural definition. It addresses itself to the routing of calls through the network, and in its most basic form it boils down to two alternatives: star or loop. Typically, in a star structure connections are made between links via the switching node. Whether the transmission equipment* (links) is cables, waveguides, radio bridges, or any other, the links radiate from the center. In a loop, there is a series connection. This results in a remarkable reduction in links and route lengths, while providing the possibility for many useful services. Examples are fault monitoring and control functions.

---

*The transmission system connecting switches to other switches and to terminals is commonly referred to as the "transmission plant."

Whether a star or loop solution is preferred, geographically separated networks must be interconnected. This is done in a hierarchical (tree) structure or in a horizontal structure. The latter has been the preferred solution, but this is changing.

Since the early years of telephony, concentration has been effected through tandem switches and links. The tandem switches have always been considered as "higher levels" in the network. The risk in a tree structure is that the time-out of a high level link will interrupt the traffic of the low levels feeding into it. Reliability is, therefore, reduced.

In an horizontal (loop or ring type) organization, signals can circulate around through alternate paths. Such an arrangement helps reduce congestion, increase traffic capacity, and, most importantly, provide for reliable solutions. As networks expand and grow, starlike, centralized solutions become bulky and prone to errors and inefficiencies. The assurance centralized solutions can provide is, very often, far less than satisfactory. Both technical and economic factors point to the wisdom of horizontal approaches.

Modularity: Horizontal networks have a significant impact in the implementation of modular solutions. While hierarchical approaches are optimized for a given level of traffic, horizontal approaches allow steady growth as the load and user requirements expand.

Software implication: A large centralized facility is very dependent on centralized control. The software is complex, difficult to maintain, and very costly.

Data base handling: A fair amount of data base activity will be provided by the architecture. The stumbling block with network solutions is the management (update, pruning, synchronization, protection) of data bases. Distributed implementation might ease the burden. (Notice, however, that data bases is the area where the jobs of the network and of the system architects interleave and interact. This is a demanding and challenging field. The communications job is not nearly as complex as data base handling.)

*Efficient journaling:** A good journal must be accurate, timely, and complete. The data must be recorded before answering processing requirements and must be available to serve reference purposes, restart, recovery, and checkpoints. The record kept must provide for checks and double checks. Procedural safeguards should assure that the record is whole, not partly written. And checks must be sufficient to weed out the junk.

Topological Solutions

The purpose of a network is to interconnect host computers and terminals so that a user of any of the DTE (or one of the entry points) has access to all other DTE on the network.

*See chapter 12.

Figure 4.1
Topology solutions

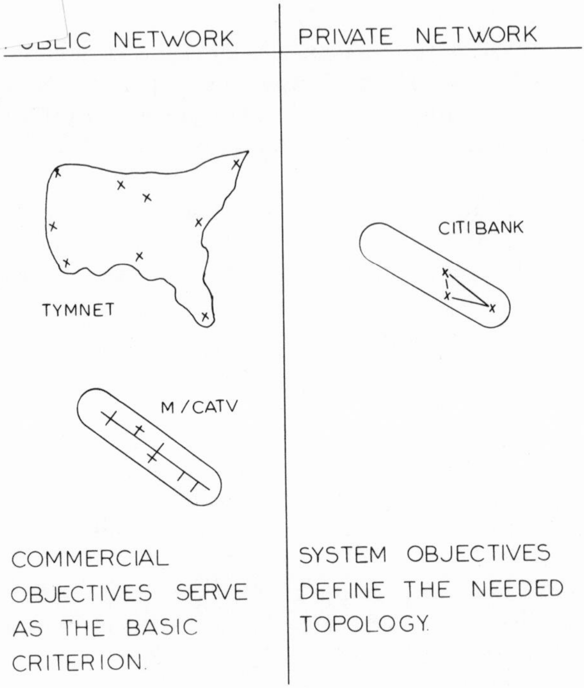

PUBLIC NETWORK	PRIVATE NETWORK
TYMNET / M/CATV	CITIBANK
COMMERCIAL OBJECTIVES SERVE AS THE BASIC CRITERION.	SYSTEM OBJECTIVES DEFINE THE NEEDED TOPOLOGY.

The design of a topological layout has two important prerequisites. The first is to start with the objectives. A topology is designed with specific objectives in mind; see Figure 4.1. The second is the appreciation of the interactive nature which exists between the topology of a network and the protocols which serve it: protocols (different by type) presuppose a topology (there is *no* standard topology) and must be chosen to *support* the topology and not to defy it.

Since the early first generation of computer networks, the switching nodes were essentially invisible to the user. As horizontal networks evolved from vertical networks and were influenced by their problems, one of the reasons for having that extra hardware was to reduce the host software costs. Without the nodes it is necessary to interface every host computer with every other host computer and to install telecommunications support in every host. With them, it is only necessary to interface each host with the node switch minicomputer and the identical minicomputers with each other, thus creating the *backbone* of the network.

By creating a backbone structure, the entire network would act as a single *data bus*. This is the solution used by Arpanet, Telenet, Tymnet, Datapac, Transpac, and Citinet. The backbone structure will care for all switching operations, including store and forward, error control, and other value-added services. It will provide the means to connect foreign devices to the lines (not available on traditional circuit switching links). It will ensure controlled redundancy to increase reliability, and will handle the generalized communications functions.

The following system elements constitute the backbone:

1. *Node switches* (usually minicomputers)
2. *Links* (bidirectional physical connection between the two nodes X and Y)
3. *Neighborhood (subset) principle* (node X is a neighbor of node Y if both X and Y are operational and connected by a physical link)
4. *Route* (This route should not be confused with the physical link. Between the nodes K and L the route is a connected sequence of operational links and nodes, starting with link K and ending with link L.)
5. *User* (a process or a job in some host)
6. *Record* (the unit of user-generated information that the network conveys from DTE A [node K] to DTE B [node L])
7. *Message* (a network-generated piece of information that travels from node K to node L)
8. *Topology change* (any one of the following events or any combination thereof: a link going down [ceasing to function]; a link coming up; a node crashing; a node restarting [by this is meant the node minicomputer, not the host])
9. *Service change* (are subject to fluctuations due to congestion control)
10. *Network control center*

Networks must be managed, that is, their operations planned, directed and controlled. Their overall performance will depend on the choices which are made in terms of planning and control.

There are no universal solutions to this subject. Some network architectures are highly centralized, for instance, IBM's SNA in its original version. Other network architectures distribute the planning, directing, and controlling functions; an excellent example is ARPA. Still other architectural solutions seek a compromise route; for instance, Tymnet has a central control point for its coast to coast network in the United States, but there are two stand-by control centers in other parts of the country, each ready to take over in case the primary one is down.

Figure 4.2 identifies the alternatives which exist between centralized and distributed environments. The alternatives bring into evidence the impact dynamically managed service tables can have on network performance.

Sender and Receiver

Topology information has a major influence on design characteristics In a network of some size, it quickly becomes quite impractical to have a direct connection between every two nodes. Thus, in order for the network to route records between nodes X and Y, it may be necessary to route these records via nodes X, U, V, and Y.

Figure 4.2
Routing table

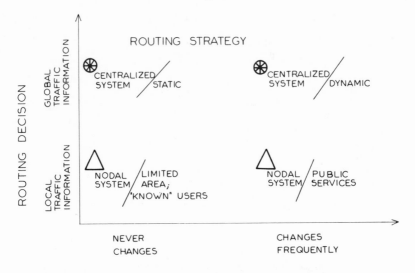

This implies that node X (the sender) must know enough about the network topology to determine that in order to get the record to node Y it should send it to node U. Node U (the intermediate) must recognize that the record is not destined for itself, but for some other node. Furthermore, node U must also know enough about the network topology to determine that in order to get the record to node Y it should send it on to node V, its neighbor. When the network topology changes, some scheme must exist whereby these changes are made known to all nodes in the network. However, the occurrence of topology changes should be invisible to the users of the network.

A DTE at node X communicating with the computer at node Y should be totally unaffected by changes (which occur while the session is "on") in the route between nodes X and Y, as long as such a route continues to exist. But if all routes between X and Y are down, the user's connection will be automatically closed and the user should be informed of what happened. The necessary information about the topology of the network is stored in routing tables. The nodes in the network inform each other about topology changes by sending each other special messages (housekeeping or netchange). All network architectures provide routines that send and receive housekeeping messages and make the appropriate changes in the routing tables.

Compared to the possible complexity presented by the overall performance of a large computers and communications network, this particular task—the actual process of record relaying (or record switching)—is a conceptually trivial one. The sender and intermediate nodes merely consult their routing tables to determine which neighboring node to send the record to. The interesting part is the scheme used to make network topology changes known to all nodes in the network. This is the job of the housekeeping protocols. Thus the problem is to design a correct topology information maintenance control and implement the protocol in question.

Because networks can get unwieldy and complex, a sound and often-used policy is to work at the subnetwork level. In order to correctly relay a record, a node does not need to know the complete and exact topology of the network. All it must know is what direction to send the record, that is, what link it should transmit the record on. In other words, it should know the identity of the first node along the route between itself and the destination node. If there are alternate, feasible routes, it needs to know the relative lengths of these routes. Length is measured in terms of "hops." Thus a route with two intermediate nodes in it is three hops long. This information can be stored in tabular form in a "distance table," which has a column for every node in the network (mapped into the node in reference). Each node has such a distance table, and it should be clear that each node's distance table is different from that of the other nodes'.

Sharing tasks

The backbone of a distributed computers and communications network is designed to take maximum advantage of available resources by sharing tasks. Sharing the communications tasks and distributing the data processing and data base requirements increases the profitability of the resources. Smaller computers working together in a distributed network can provide high responsiveness at each local computer and large system power at a reduced cost. In addition to speed and cost advantages, this type of network gains by its modular construction. Any increased need can be met directly, without necessarily upgrading other network parts.

With high-speed, broad bandwidth data communications available, the system itself will determine how and where processing is done and storage maintained. Operators will make fewer decisions as "secure" operating systems take complete control of the system resources.

Ease of use is perhaps the number one objective and can be attained as the Arpanet, Tymnet, Datapac, Cyclades, and Citinet (among others) experiences demonstrate. In turn, these facilities see to it that more on-line communication oriented systems will evolve as these facilities become easier to use, privacy and security concepts are proven, and systems become more reliable and dependable.

Five characteristics in support of end-user objectives in the coming decade can be distinguished.

The first is distributed special-function processors, including instruction stream processors, file processors, communication processors, event processors, and supervisor processors.

The second characteristic is interpretive processing capability both for end use and for developmental activities. For the program development environment, high-level microprogrammed minicomputers will execute source code (such as PL/1, Cobol, Fortran, and APL) directly.

Figure 4.3

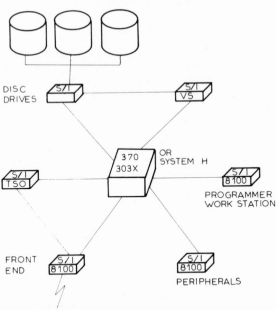

Figure 4.3 demonstrates a hexagonal structure which in the early 1980s might constitute IBM's strategy and the plug compatible manufacturer's dilemma. The minicomputers are dedicated machines—one per task. The tasks are identified. In a sense, this is a local network development—the way we discussed it in the beginning of this chapter.

"Native node" minicomputers will be available for performance-conscious, production-oriented users. Indeed, this may become a competitive strategy both for computer manufacturers and for major users.

Memory hierarchy is the third characteristic. Most hosts and DTEs will utilize their own private high-speed cache (buffers) as well as up to 256,000 characters of integrated main memory, and will be able to share a larger (over 100 million characters) secondary or bulk storage. Communications will be increasingly bit oriented. (In this context, it should be noted that the word bytes has been dropped from most IBM 370 documents, and the System/80 "character" may be defined on a dynamic basis, i.e., consisting of 4, 8, n bits, depending on the function to be performed.)

The fourth characteristic is that high-speed, wideband bus will be the basic medium, probably as optical fibers. No one thinks anymore of making a star connection. All the local system resources will exchange data and communicate with each other via a unique wideband, multiaccess bus.

Figure 4.4

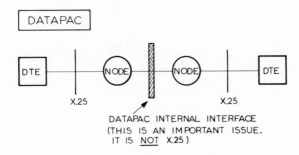

DATAPAC

X.25   X.25

DATAPAC INTERNAL INTERFACE
(THIS IS AN IMPORTANT ISSUE.
IT IS <u>NOT</u> X.25)

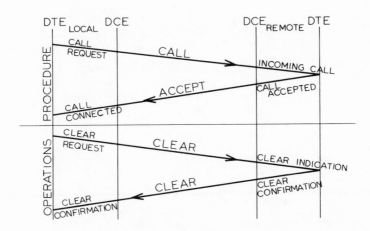

The fifth characteristic is that input–output interconnections will take new forms. A single, multiplexed wire (coaxial cable) or loop (dual loops will be optional for redundancy) operating at a very high speed will probably replace today's numerous cables. This loop system will also permit, in effect, replacing the "channel" function with special integrated input–output processors.

At the network level, monitoring centers will be provided, with the functions to support diagnostic information and inform on error conditions. The services to be offered include line quality monitoring, remote tests, control of configuration, and remote control of software.

New facilities will evolve, such as port sharing and port selection. Communication equipment has a cost proportioned to the number of ports; hence, we don't wish to dedicate ports to suppliers.

High-speed bus adapters will probably be the means by which mainframes will

Figure 4.5
Alternative 1 (*e.g., may be a program which makes the MF look like a terminal—Case Datapoint/6600)

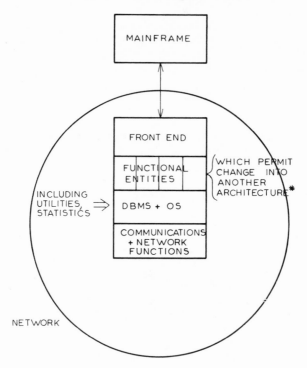

connect to front ends and peripherals. Internet gateway computers will also be provided and this represents a whole *new* type of technology.

Datapac—An example of Network Service

The Canadian Datapac—one of the first packet-switching networks to come into service—is internally structured as a number of distinct layers. Each of them provides a set of communication facilities.

The outer three layers are packet subnet, virtual circuit (or liaison) process layer, and subscriber access (or interface service) layer. Protocol choice and message handling are shown in Figure 4.4.

The packet subnet provides facilities for a process in one node to send or receive packets to or from processes in another node. This layer uses the internal nodal trunks, together with a routing strategy and a defined packet format. The packet subnet does not guarantee that packets will be delivered in sequence without loss or duplication. It does, however, guarantee that the data field of packets that are

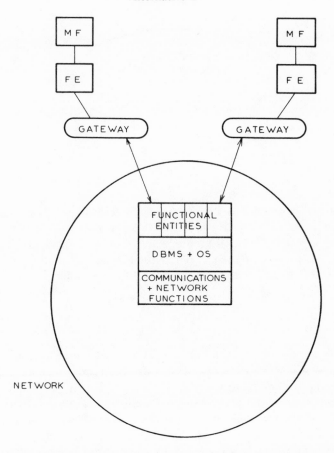

Figure 4.6
Alternative 2

delivered is correct. The properties of the packet subnet arise from such factors as the use of alternate routing for packets between nodes when there are parallel facilities or, in cases of failure, retransmission (when errors are detected). The trunks employ a link protocol designed to detect errors in transmission and invoke packet retransmission when any errors are detected.

The main function of the virtual circuit layer is to set up flow control and end-to-end error control schemes to handle the traffic between pairs of processors or processes. Flow control is achieved by the receiver controlling the "credits" that it sends to the transmitter. This is determined by the rate at which packets are "consumed" by the receiving terminal. End-to-end error control is responsible for resequencing, duplicate detection, and recovery from packet loss. Recovery is effected by the sending node holding a copy of each packet that it has sent until an acknowledgement is received. When a packet is sent from the local node to the

Figure 4.7

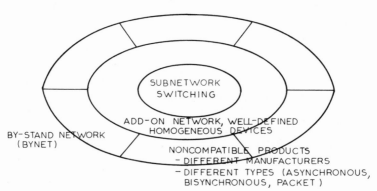

remote node, a copy of the packet is kept and a timer is started. If the remote node receives the packet correctly, it returns a positive acknowledgment. If the acknowledgment is not received before the timer expires, then the local node will retransmit the packet. After a specific number of retransmissions, the call is aborted.

Finally, the subscriber access layer leads into session and presentation control.

Gateways

An important service of Datapac and of all advanced user-oriented data communications networks is the capability to interface disciplines other than the primary one which they support, for instance, asynchronous and bisynchronous within a packet-switching environment. Datapac does that with the so-called network interface machine (NIM). Stated differently, the user's DTEs (computers, terminal controllers, terminals) may be connected directly to the Datapac network using point-to-point links. DTEs not capable of implementing the Datapac protocol, for instance, point-of-sale terminals, would be connected to the NIMS.

Present data services are based upon providing a physical data channel, a dedicated bandwidth. This may be permanently leased as a private line or periodically accessed as a switched offering. But the crucial issue is the provision of gateways which permit different line disciplines to be attached to the network.

The Datapac solution is one possible alternative. In general, publicly offered data communications services must choose between two alternatives, as presented in figures 4.5 and 4.6, respectively.

Alternative 1 calls for the network to provide a wide variety of services from front ends to mainframes. This is seconded by internal gateway capabilities (functional entities) and by the other services the network must offer. Stated briefly, a gateway is a path offered between two information processing systems with dissimilar protocols. It provides the necessary transformation from one protocol to the other—and thus allows the exchange of information.

Alternative 2 leaves the front ending to the client, dividing the gateway between an internal and an external part, the former being the more important. Point-of-sales equipment, for instance, can be front ended by an intelligent concentrator whose functions would include the conversion of an asynchronous protocol to that of the network, though the network may also choose to offer some of these conversion functions.

A third possibility is to project the network in three layers; see Figure 4.7. The central one, subnetwork/switching, will be the true backbone. This is the case of the CIGAL subnetwork in the Cyclades network. An external layer will basically consist of gateways. It will be built up as user requirements develop. Between the internal and the external, there is an intermediate layer which is dedicated to the service of well-defined, homogenous devices conforming to the network's dominant protocol.

5

Cost-Benefit with the New Technologies

We have been discussing distributed information systems as an overall term for a variety of processing structures whose common goal is the placement of local computer power at the disposal of every unit of business. The purposes have been described as enhancing each unit's operations, controlling a timely flow of intelligence among these units, and reducing data-handling costs.

Every phase of data processing has a cost in time and in money; both must be accounted for along with the conceptual integrity of the system determining its ease of use. In terms of time, money, and intervening errors, the cost is higher the further out the sources and the destination of the data; see Figure 5.1

This is why the traditional batch-processing channel did not work well. In a batch-processing environment data is grouped in order to be transmitted in the same data-handling operation. The disadvantages are obvious: delays, costs, and errors. At the point of origin, clerical hours are spent in the transcribing, batching, and expediting of the support media (usually paper) to the central location. Then time will be spent on data-entry equipment; computer runs will be needed to weed out errors; more clerical time will be required to check the computer outputs; and a sequential treatment is necessary to update files: the operating system launches the program on the basis of job control cards.

This operation is obsolete, slow, and clumsy. We have available today the methodology and the systems necessary for moving information from a *source* location to the *processing* sites and on to the *destination*. Modern technology provides a set of functions necessary for the manipulation of the *input* information to produce the desired *output* (results) and this can be done on-line.

Getting On-Line

One of the biggest breakthroughs in data processing has been the development of the on-line access terminal. For the first time management has data that is up to the

53

Figure 5.1

Computer use on an integrated basis should start at point of origin (as early as possible) and end at point of destination (as late as feasible). Only then can computer use give profitable results.

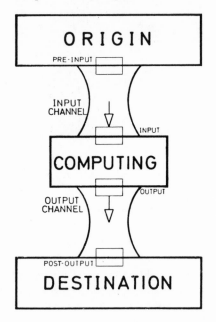

minute. Today, the on-line method is the basic design of a whole new generation of inexpensive computers. Forward-looking industries and financial institutions are using them for better management control and more efficient operation throughout decisions issues, scheduling processes, and settlement procedures; see Figure 5.2.

A description of the elements which define a distributed information system distinguishes four basic aspects:

Distributed processing at transaction level

Distributed communications (not only transmission)

Distributed data bases

Distributed procedures (restructured to fit the organizational requirements and to profit from the new technological realities)

The days when state-of-the-art limitations forced users to place all their computer resources at a distant central site are past. There is today no reason for adjusting business operations to meet the restrictions imposed by such centralization.

Distribution of computer power is made feasible by technology in a way that best fits the user's needs by locating processing and storage capabilities *close* to the

Figure 5.2
Information handling in an organization can be divided into three large families of problems

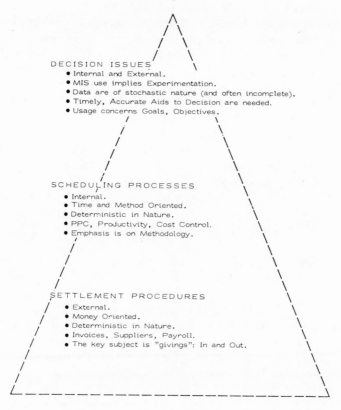

DECISION ISSUES
- Internal and External.
- MIS use implies Experimentation.
- Data are of stochastic nature (and often incomplete).
- Timely, Accurate Aids to Decision are needed.
- Usage concerns Goals, Objectives.

SCHEDULING PROCESSES
- Internal.
- Time and Method Oriented.
- Deterministic in Nature.
- PPC, Productivity, Cost Control.
- Emphasis is on Methodology.

SETTLEMENT PROCEDURES
- External.
- Money Oriented.
- Deterministic in Nature.
- Invoices, Suppliers, Payroll.
- The key subject is "givings": In and Out.

workplace: the individual office at headquarters, the factory floor, the sales or inventory management outlet, or the branch office. Whether on-line terminals or minicomputers are installed at remote locations, it becomes feasible to:

1. Shorten the data input route
2. Avoid repetitive clerical operations
3. Provide for error detection and protection as the data is captured and transcribed
4. Improve the response time
5. Eliminate the delay inherent in round trips
6. Assure an interactive type of man-machine communication
7. Reduce the costs of data handling
8. Simplify programming tasks and handle more transaction in the process
9. Automate the fringes of the operations in the periphery—which so far have defied computers

The organizational study and the definition of the logical functions are the pillars on which a good solution will rest.

One reason for distributed networks not becoming widespread overnight is that the currently installed base of computer systems is primarily centralized and batch oriented. That investment in equipment and software cannot be lightly tossed aside and will continue in place until depreciated. In fact, the solution adopted by the Bank of America is an excellent example of this policy. It explores the capabilities of DIS and puts into action a range of possibilities while it enhances past investments in the maxicomputer class.

Another basic reason why DIS has not become widespread overnight is the lack of images in the minds of both analysts and users with which to explore the new frontiers. A terminal for each user is an efficient solution which quite often makes economic sense. But where will the drive come from to put into action departures from the past which often negate what people have been taught to believe whether formally or through personal experience?

Decentralization and Centralization

Like its organizational counterpart, the decentralization of computer equipment is not an easy task. Distributed processing can represent a compromise between centralized and decentralized processing, accounting for the issue of human effectiveness versus system efficiency (i.e., hardware performance per dollar versus people productivity), and corporate issues and current practices such as the use of centralized information systems—now a vital part of the headquarters' management—functioning in today's decentralized organizational management. Information requirements are best answered through a transition, rather than by a total negation of current facts.

Because control over information means greater political power, the corporation and its organizational subentities are increasingly dependent on data processing systems. This makes availability and reliability of the information resources, a critical issue. This used to be the case in some industries (e.g., airlines), but by now it is widespread—the whole financial sector being a specific case.

On the other hand, it is just as true that data processing's growing percentage of total budgets is causing corporations to seek means to optimize their computer expenses while caring for and feeding this vital resource. While the larger organizations look for economics and for alternatives, technological improvements and developments such as microprocessors, minicomputers, and input–output devices mean that smaller company organizational units can now afford their own equipment. The classic accounting machine gives way to the minicomputer at least, to the sophisticated terminal systems with full processing capabilities.

But management also has other concerns to look after: security of information system resources when centralized sites are possible targets of dissident groups is a factor in some decisions to distribute the corporation's nerve center and data bases.

The decentralization of information systems is no eccentricity on the behalf of organizations. It is a hard fact of life. Security, privacy, even survival may depend on it.

Facing the Constraints

We can say easily that of all the constraints and factors involved, hardware represents one of the least important, whereas software and management issues are very significant, perhaps even paramount.

The evolution toward DIS passed through the phase of centralized real-time operations. This left its mark on present-day systems. Of the systems labeled as distributed, many prove to be centralized data bases that have been divided among several sites.

A recent survey revealed the following statistics among the companies interviewed. Users of truly distributed systems accounted for only 30 percent of the population surveyed. Some 20 percent of the computer users planned to split their data bases among several remote locations. But 35 percent had definitely decided against that option, while the reremainder had no specifics worked out for an eventual distributed systems plan. The survey also found that exactly half the users intended to install a terminal-based system, if they had not done so already, and that 35 percent planned to acquire at least one minicomputer-based system.

Only one of the users interviewed rejected distributed processing outright after thoroughly evaluating the alternatives. Other users, however, were undecided about the approach either because they suspected that distributed processing would clash with their existing procedures or because their data processing plans were still in the formative stage.

However, it is a common weakness of surveys that they fail to identify the transition concepts in management thinking as new systems and components arise. Delay in application is directly related to this transition.

The first big move was made not in the 1970s but in the 1950s with the transition from punched card (unit record) equipment to computers. Such equipment was so deeply imbedded in thinking—both among specialists and at the management level—that it dominated computer usage until practically today. We can only hope that this sort of failure will not repeat itself with DIS—treating minicomputers as large-scale equipment.

The next major transition took place with the move from reasonably small to big machines, naturally for reasons of cost effectiveness.

Finally we now realize how inefficient we are with big systems. We tried for too long and too hard to run the big machines like small ones. We found out the hard way that even scale has its diseconomics: you have to keep the system running, find experienced operators, and hire more people. All this costs so much more money. And software costs outrun the user's budget. This is the problem with project management; it is made for the small, sharp team of experts. Man-made software is also too slow and not big enough for large-scale computer systems. As a result, the systems profession is retooling for new horizons where the impact of the computer will be felt to its fullest extent.

Computers must make their own software—or at least assist the expert in constructing it on-line. Hardware interfaces, controllers, peripherals, and communications devices must be studied in detail. They should have sufficient intelligence to enable timely hook-ups and plug-to-plug compatibility. A plug-to-plug compatibility goal for both hardware and software will enable capitalizing on the coming technical breakthroughs in mass memories, data communications, and a range of peripherals. Plug-to-plug compatible software can and should be attained. Most importantly, we must make the machine (terminal, front-end, local minicomputer) work unattended. If in a network, we must assure that the power is kept on so that a host computer can call it automatically.

The human elements are the most vital but also the most expensive components of the information system. We should be thrifty in the use of clerical help in general and of the computer operators in particular—but not when it comes to putting systems talent to work.

Criteria for Choice

One of the subjects which the current literature leaves unexplained is the criteria for choosing minicomputers and related equipment when confronted with a specific choice. This lack of guidelines leads to difficulties which are compounded by the fact that minicomputers are predominantly installed near operating entities—while operating entities dislike becoming involved in matters of technology, including programming, operations, standards, and communications.

Below is a list of criteria for evaluating alternative approaches and guidelines compiled from visits with leading American and European financial institutions.*

If the minicomputer is projected for use in multiple installations (e.g., branch offices, factories, sales offices), then choose only one type of equipment.

If the machine is to be used only for *one* installation (e.g., foreign operations, commercial paper, the management of a large client), then choose the equipment with the characteristics which indicate the best way of tackling the job.

The software accompanying the machine should always be considered, but its availability is much more crucial where the machine will be used for only one installation.

There should be no more than one basic application on the minicomputer at any time, unless the applications are very similar. A multiprocessing environment should be avoided.

The creation (and, hence, proliferation) of peripheral data processing centers,

---

*Citibank, Bank of America, and First National Bank of Boston in the United States; Paribas, Lafarge, and the author's own experiences in Europe are the basic background references.

in the classic way we know them, is an expensive mistake. There should be *no* minicenters, no professional operators.

The minicomputer software should be written at the center, but a wise policy is to allow for "user exits" and to let it be known that contributions are welcomed. Periodically, these should be examined and pruned.

Site selection should be evaluated in the light of service both to the branch and to the organization. The proper topology can make it feasible that less than 20 percent of the operations in the periphery interest the center, and less than 2 percent touch other regions. (the 80/20 rule).

The justification of a minicomputer installation should definitely respond to basic economics. Some organizations adopted the rule that a branch with 50 people or more should be a minicomputer site.

It is just as good to say that saving the wages of one and a half employees justifies the installation of a minicomputer. Bread-and-butter financial criteria are the most solid cornerstones to a decision.

Table 5.1 presents a cost comparison between a batch job and a German industrial firm. Two procedures are considered and each costed on a maxicomputer and a minicomputer. The difference is striking. For the same applications, the ratio between maxicomputer and minicomputer yearly costs is 2.97:1. Fringe benefits, for example, easier access, are at the minicomputer's side.

Table 5.1

Cost Comparison of a Batch Job from a German Industrial Firm

	Cost (1,000 Deutsche marks, KDM)	
	Procedure I	*Procedure II*
Maxicomputer		
Hardware	160	45
Operational expenses	130 ⌐	36
Supplies	150	56
Data entry	220	36
	660	173
	⌐ 833 KDM/YEAR	
Minicomputer		
Hardware	140	40
Operational expenses	30 ⌐	10
Supplies	20	10
Different expenses and reserve	(20	10)
	210	70
	└ 280 KDM/YEAR	

Table 5.2

Cost Comparison of a Maxicomputer and a Minicomputer in a Real-time
Environment

Service	Maxicomputer Starlike Network	Minicomputer
1. Central processor	Rental $$\frac{\$100,000/m}{250\ T} = \$400/m, T$$	Purchase $$\frac{\$110,000}{5\ \text{years}} = \$2,000/\text{year for 7 terminals}$$
2. Terminals	Purchase $$\frac{\$10,000/\text{year}}{5Y} = \$2,000/Y, T$$	
3. Lines	$$\frac{\$600,000/\text{year}}{250\ T} = \$2,400/Y, T$$	At 1/5 this cost x 7 (for 7 terminals) = $3,360/year
4. Operations expenses	Take 100% of central processor expenses: $4,800/Y,T	Must be nil but, say, 1/4 of 1 man-year, at $24,000/man-year = $6,000/year
Summary	$14,000/Y.T for 7 terminals = $98,000/year	$31,360/year
5. Client service		+
6. Reliability/availability		+
7. Software development and maintenance		+

Key: m = month
   Y = year
   T = terminal

Now look at a real-time environment; Table 5.2 gives the data. It compares a minicomputer installation's ability to handle seven terminals in a bank's branch office to a starlike network's ability. Here the cost ratio between maxicomputer and minicomputer is greater: 3.12:1. In addition to financial benefits, the minicomputer provides better client service, reliability/availability, and software development and maintenance.

A leading financial institution adopted the following rule for the justification of a minicomputer at a branch office: The small branch office with seven or eight people will have a terminal, and offices with ten to twelve people will have a small minicomputer. The bigger branch office with thirty or more people will have a minicomputer with terminals connecting other branch offices. A solid rule underscores the economic facts. The savings of one or two people justifies the installation financially. A properly used minicomputer in a major branch or department can easily save up to four persons while absorbing the extra work.

Cost issues with Future Systems

Organizations with DIS experience are quick to emphasize that such systems must be powerful and flexible enough to meet users' current needs and that they should have sufficient expansion capacity to provide for future needs.

System planners should look for:

1. Provision for standalone and clustered terminal configurations
2. Multitasking to allow more than one terminal at a remote location to access the same data base at the same time
3. Concurrency (but not multiprocessing) to allow more than one job, such as data entry, hard copy, or video communications, to be performed at the same time

Such points are just as valid whether they concern a local, multipoint, or network environment served by minicomputers. To the above list should be added:

1. Ability to dedicate the system to one large application
2. Choice of hardware which can be expanded in the field
3. Ability to handle variable storage capacities (large and small files)
4. Availability of multiple methods of accessing locally stored files, including simple sequential, indexed, or direct access
5. System security provisions including the ability to prevent access to individual fields in a record, individual records or files, individual terminals, or access to specific commands.

Optional choice of technical factors may be invalidated through the wrong use of economic criteria. As always, the major issue is cost.

If we wish to take advantage of the possibilities which present-day technology makes feasible, namely, the distribution of computer power in a way that best fits the user's needs, we must be on the look out for the bottomless pits which absorb money—programs and data bases. These are the two areas where the highest costs lie. The interests of future buyers and sellers will center here. The pertinent factors in these areas must be carefully studied and analyzed. Available resources must be optimized and shared to the fullest possible extent. The degree to which a careful, well-implemented study can change yesterday's economic or operational criteria is often surprising.

The selection of a programming language is important to users both during and after system development, since the time and costs involved in programming can exceed those involved in hardware implementation. Users are well advised to look for fully implemented interactive language capabilities, industry standard high-level language if available, the ability to use different languages if need be, and programmability down to the single terminal level.

Then, to economize on the data base side, users should appreciate that it is not sufficient enough to locate the processing and storage capabilities close to the workplace—the office at headquarters, the factory floor, the sales and inventory outlet, or the branch office—but they must also

1. Rethink the data bases
2. Shorten the data input route
3. Provide for error detection and correction
4. Improve the response time
5. Eliminate the delay inherent in round trips
6. Ensure interactive man-machine communication
7. Handle more transactions in the process
8. Automate the fringes of the operations in the periphery—which so far defied the computers
9. Simplify the programming tasks
10. Study maintainability in advance and allow the basic system to evolve toward larger configurations
11. Ensure that future developments will safeguard the software made today

In regard to this last aspect, as management becomes keener to automate clerical jobs and to shorten the path to decision, the cost is often paid in an accelerated obsolescence of the software. By putting the user directly into the picture, on-line solutions may help increase both the portability and the longevity of the computer programs.

Growth Curves

Over the last twenty-five years of computer use we often lost sight of the fact that hardware and even software are not the really dominant issues in establishing and running computerized solutions. The real problems are organizational and psychological ones.

For on-line approaches to be successful, the overriding need is to study, quantify, and convince. Planning tasks are a prerequisite. The seven major steps in this planning process are:

1. Determine current work load of the data center
2. Determine future work load requirements
3. Define work load capacity and performance of current configuration (hardware and software)
4. Define projected (required) capacity and performance of minicomputer configuration (hardware and software)
5. Determine user response times and other production requirements
6. Determine overall minicomputer site performance criteria
7. Determine planned costs and performance of the minicomputer site

Figure 5.3
Projected transaction load, and software/hardware throughput

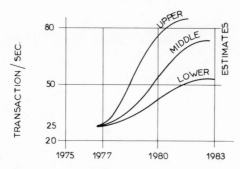

As the data load at the computer site grows, will transactions per second be handled better through many minis, a few midi, or one maxi location? A functional distribution makes it practical to implement large applications. Adding to a central location increases the load of transactions per second and most likely worsens the response time. What is the projected growth in requirements if user demands are given free reign?

A 1977 study examined just that. The current on-line rate of 25 transactions per second (Figure 5.3) was projected over a six-year period, requiring that the information processed at corporate headquarters be entered in widely dispersed geographic locations. Such processing included source data entry including error correction ability, local data storage needs, retrieval, interrogations (both local and centralized), and remote job entry. In addition, the projected systems should provide extensive operating utilities along with consistent and accurate access to data bases at remote locations.

In the study it was management's choice that orders and general information should be entered daily through its network of sales offices. Manufacturing plants must enter customers' order acknowledgments, shipping information, and inter-plant orders. Data should be transmitted automatically between local processing centers to reduce the cost of human operators. In addition, personnel transactions, sales and marketing data, credit checking, and inventory status had to be performed through the same system. The mission given to the designers was to project an integrated applications-oriented system.

This led to the estimate which Figure 5.3 exemplifies: implementation of the system will more than double the current transaction rate over the next three years as priority is given to larger operating units, while over the following three years, transactions will grow at a lower pace, accounting for the smaller offices being automated and for normal business growth as well.

The network study made in connection with management policy also led to the establishment of selection criteria. Minicomputers should be capable of integrating technological advances in the area of data communications: provide an industry-

Figure 5.4

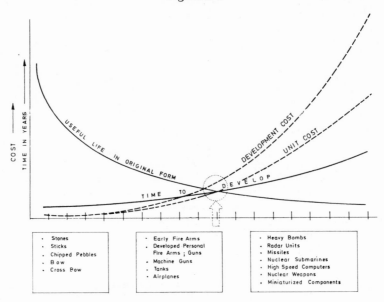

standard formal set of conventions, provide terminal-to-terminal communications, be compatible with and committed to eventual implementation of X.25, provide both auto-dial and auto-answer capabilities to allow automatic polling of data from unattended remote locations, and ensure downline software loading to permit control of a distributed system from a central location.

Lessons Learned

We can now integrate into a comprehensive list the lessons to be learned and the advantages to be derived from on-line processing made feasible through cheaper technology and the advent of distributed information systems.

Comparative lower costs of components will alter historical design rules, since the price cuts will be industrywide and widespread. The "new" systems will substitute through electronics the functions now performed by more expensive methods, including those performed through people.

The spate of new product announcements will continue and, with it, the market will expand. It went from 50 systems in 1953 to 175,000 in 1977. By 1985 there will be at least one installation in *every* American company with over 50 people. The number of installed terminals of all types, which exceeded one million in 1975, will continue to grow by 30 to 40 percent a year.

Approximately 60 to 65 percent of all systems will use some kind of communications facility, devices or lines, by the end of this year. By 1980 it is estimated that some 85 percent of all systems installed will be communications oriented. The overwhelming trend will be that of soft copy (CRT) use, with many computer installations moving away from hard copy; on-line capabilities will accelerate this trend.

The research and development budget for hardware development, software construction, data communications research, and applications evolution will increase sharply. For hardware and software only, $2 billion annually is a conservative figure for the United States. Figure 5.4 gives a glimpse of R + D expenditures as man-made systems move further away from the Stone Age.

Volume is a good measure of where the R + D money goes. In the early 1950s, a 650 would have occupied 400 ft³ if 1 megabyte were available. By 1962 (with 7070 and 360/30) this volume was reduced to 100 ft³. By 1972 (with the 370/135 and 145) it went down to 8 ft³. By 1975 it further decreased to 0.5 ft³. The ratio is 0.5/400 = 1/800 in 20 years! It is anticipated that with 16,000 chips as the workhorse it will take only 0.063 ft³ for 1 megabyte and the ratio will be

$$\frac{0.063}{400} = \frac{1.57}{10,000} = \frac{1}{6.370}$$

Equally impressive is the drop in disc storage: from 5 megabytes in the late 1950s to 400 megabytes with IBM's 3350, or 5/400 = 1/80 in 20 years without appreciable change in volumes.

Before the end of the decade, among computer manufacturers the hardware will look alike and will be inexpensive. What they will be selling is systems software, programmed applications, and expertise. Computer manufacturers now spend much more on software than on hardware development. Thus it is logical that they will derive more income from their know-how. This means that the computer user should expect to pay dearly for software and services. It is better to be aware of this now, rather than later.

New applications developments may have been the bottleneck in the last decade, and as Professor Schmidt* said: "The bottleneck is always at the top of the bottle." In fact, the growth of the market will be limited more severely by the lack of knowledge. This is just as true of the capacity to process data on-line.

---

*Formerly chief executive officer of Brown Bovery, Germany, and Board Member of Nestle.

6

Basic Definitions for Architectural Design

We shall begin this subject by providing the needed background, explaining the esoteric terms and definitions, and treating the fundamentals.

As applied to the framework of distributed information systems, an architecture is a set of functions, interfaces, and protocols. It provides a structure and a framework to do task-to-task, end-to-end, job-to-job, and the overall data communications processes with accuracy, adaptability, and reliability. To accomplish basic aims, the architectural design should consider the topology, the applications environment, the hardware to be used, and the software which is available or under development. Invariably, the architecture will have to provide for (1) device-sharing—integrating machines (hardware) and running routines; (2) file-sharing—including data base management system DBMS) aspects; and (3) the operating systems functions. This is what the architecture of Arpanet, Telenet, Tymnet, and other data communications networks operating at the moment is doing.

Overall, the architecture will be divided into communications, networking, and applications. To cover its functions it must account for control actions to be applied to messages, transport, paths, links, and errors. The architecture must also contribute to the data base and applied programming routines, including file access, DBMS, programming library, operating system functions, and possibly encryption. Such functions clearly underline the fact that the development of a systems—or a network—architecture calls not only for *concepts* but for a *whole mechanism* as well to be put into action.

Systems Architecture and Network Architecture

Why is there a distinction between "systems" architecture and "network" architecture? Because functional differences exist between them.

67

In terms of architectural design a distinction must be drawn between network architecture and distributed systems. Distributed processing, for instance, may be all in one physical location; this is the Bank of America's solution in its present implementation. The network architecture will start at that point and go into the environment. This architecture, which might support 1,000 terminals or more, is *outside* the "internal" module devoted to processing purposes.

It is possible to enlarge the framework presented in this specific example by establishing a definition which can pass the test of time as concepts evolve and new systems develop. A systems architecture for DIS may cover distributed processing and, to a substantial degree, distributed data bases, but it does *not* need to provide a network solution. Two facts characterize this approach: (1) The minicomputers (say, the work stations) at the periphery (and even at the headquarters) will not necessarily be linked together into a network projected and implemented by the user—including its nodes, lines, and software support. * (2) The on-line operation between work stations will take place sometimes during the day but *not* continuously—a condition which would have required a network approach.

The solution which Paribas has adopted is a cost-effective one using the state of the art in systems technology to the best advantage and is an example of systems architecture.

The solution Citibank has chosen with its privately owned CITINET is an example of network architecture. (Citibank hired a specialized firm to build the network as a result of the experience of ARPA.) Public networks—Telenet, Tymnet, Datapac, Transpac—have to go through network architecture, but not all users need to follow Citibank solution. Value-added carriers will, to a very large extent, make this unnecessary.

A network architecture is the only one that can ensure distributed operating systems, on-line maintenance, and end-to-end encryption. But not all users have the expertise to set up the system on their own, and most manufacturers are still in the developmental stages of this advanced discipline.

Not only is it important to distinguish between network architecture and systems architecture, but also the user must be brought into the picture from the start. The information-centered computer and communications systems we have been discussing make this a necessity. In Table 6.1 ten critical issues are outlined, and user interaction with the network and with the systems architects is shown for each of these issues.

Within a systems architecture it will be required to specify all the functions that exist at the level of the projected DIS implementation. Generally, it will not be necessary to design the interfaces between functions, say, of the same node of the network, since this should be provided by the network architecture which the user will adopt.

The systems architect must bear in mind software configurations, equipment selection, operating system explosion into discrete modules specific to certain functions, procedural developments for implementation, compatibility and trans-

*Though the latter may be provided by the computer manufacturer.

Table 6.1

User Interaction with System Architects and with Network Architects

User's Viewpoint	Systems Architect	Network Architect
1. Structural description	◄————————►	
2. Applications overview	◄————————►	
3. Network overview	◄———————————————————————►	
4. Potential systems development	◄————————►	
5. Actual examples	◄————————► ◄———————————————————————►	
6. Effects of commands on network behavior	◄———————————————————————►	
7. Communications issues	◄————————► ◄———————————————————————►	
8. Efficiency characteristics	◄————————►	
9. Design impact: changes aftermaths	◄————————►	
10. Costs	◄————————►	

parency in application modules, and maintainability of the same—and of the network—in terms of on-line tests and on-line dispositions. In this sense, systems architecture is what tomorrow's user will need most. However, to project DIS systems effectively, the user must know the data communications jargon (even its fine print) and must understand how a network works.*

The Nodes of a Network

The pivot points of a network architecture are the *nodes*. By definition, a node is any of the computer equipment connected by physical links. *It is an addressable entity.*

In other terms, all computers are nodes, independently of the function they perform. A node may be a switch, host, or terminal concentrator. A *switch* is a node which serves only the routing function. A *host* is a node able to support application programs; it is an information processor which provides supporting services to users, communicates with users, communicates with other nodes (switches, hosts), and

---

*In different terms, the know-how on a network architecture must be available even though the user may limit his design at the level of a systems architecture.

Figure 6.1

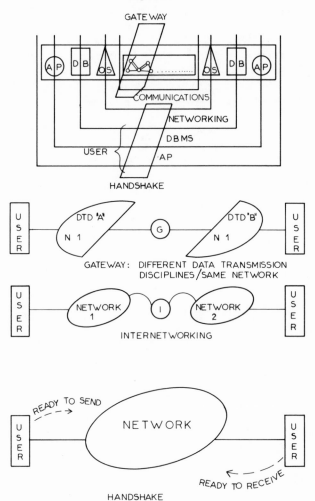

GATEWAY: DIFFERENT DATA TRANSMISSION
DISCIPLINES/SAME NETWORK

INTERNETWORKING

HANDSHAKE

offers supporting services to other hosts when necessary. A terminal concentrator is a minicomputer or microcomputer whose job is to coordinate a number of terminal devices.

Let us also add that the physical placement of a node within a network does not determine what its function is. The function is determined by what it does.

Other subjects which need to be defined in terms of network architecture are the following:

Protocols and interfaces (transparent or virtual)

Handshaking and gateways

Figure 6.2

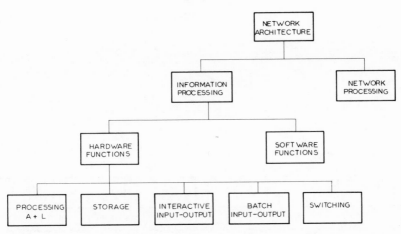

Virtual (or logical) circuits and datagrams

Streams and windows

Rejection and abort procedures

Native commands and network primitives

Downline loading and upline dumping

Balanced (symmetric) and unbalanced (asymmetric) networks

Topological layout

Performance criteria and standardization

Basic Definitions

The most critical issue following the definition of an architecture is that of protocols. Protocols interest the network as a whole, the communications subnets, and the subscribers, and they must be respected by all parties. A *protocol is a formal set of conventions governing the format and control of data.* It comprises well-defined procedures clearly understood by all parties. The data communication rules established through a protocol are applicable between similar processes. (In contrast, an interface establishes rules for communication between dissimilar processes.)

A *transparent protocol* sends data through the system without particular constraints from low-level details.* The user can't see it, but it *is* there. With a

---

*That is, protocols and standards interesting lower levels, such as the data communication equipment (modem).

Figure 6.3

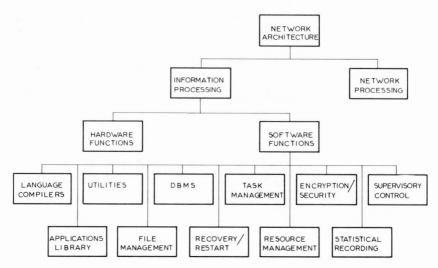

virtual protocol there is a sequence to be observed. It is better to have transparent protocols, but is is not easy.

The interfaces, too, can vary. They may be virtual or real.

A *handshake is a controlled transfer of information between the sender and the receiver.* It is ready to send and ready to receive (Figure 6.1), and as such it involves data, receipt of acknowledgments, sending completed, and completion of acknowledgment.

A *gateway is a path provided between two different data transmission disciplines, within the same network, with dissimilar protocols.* The object of the gateway is to allow the exchange of information by providing the necessary transformation from one protocol to another.

A *virtual circuit is a point-to-point switched (or permanent) circuit over which data, reset, interrupt, and flow-control packets transmit.* It is also referred to as "logical circuit" or "logical path." It is correct to observe that the virtual circuit concept defies the known principle of Euclidean geometry—that "the straight line is the shortest path between two points." Within a data communications network the shortest (or best) path is the one which is reliable and available at the same time.

A *datagram is a section of a message (typically of 256 or 512 characters) individually routed through a packet-switching network.* Datagrams are used to split long packets into smaller units. However, as compared to long remote batch transmission types (as we know them today), datagram service charges are two to four times the corresponding cost of bucket transmission because of the cost of headers, tailers, and routing. Such costs may become increasingly substantial.

A *stream is a virtual circuit application* (particularly used with reference to satellites, going through a single broadcast.)

A *window is a logical path to be opened between two processes before data can be passed*. It is used in flow control management.

The *rejection* and *abort* procedures to be adopted are very important in data communications. *Abort is invoked by the sender causing the recipient to discard (and ignore) all bit sequences transmitted by the same sender since the preceding flag sequence*. Aborting should be followed by retransmission. A good retransmission strategy is to wait a while, and if nothing comes back then retransmit. The alternative to this is to send the receiver station a NAK (*no* acknowledgment). NAK has its own problems, though, for instance, loss of its own data.

The next definition is that of *native commands* which means *native to the particular set, or subset, of an operating system*. Another way to look at native commands is to say that they are supported by an operating system, that is, they are the normally visible instructions.

Network primitives are the set of basic commands characterizing the network architecture and its subsets.

We said earlier that the implementation of a network architecture calls for a whole mechanism to be put into action. Downline loading and upline dumping are two gears of this mechanism. *Downline loading means the load of programs for immediate or deferred execution on a minicomputer or generally a network component. Upline loading, or as it is usually called, upline dumping, means sending information upline not for execution but for analysis purposes*. Both terms stem from the traditional hierarchical networks with a host (master) to satellite relationship.

We have just mentioned the traditional host (master) to satellite relationship. A *protocol which supports master/slave (or primary/secondary) computer operations is called unbalanced or asymmetric.*

Figure 6.4

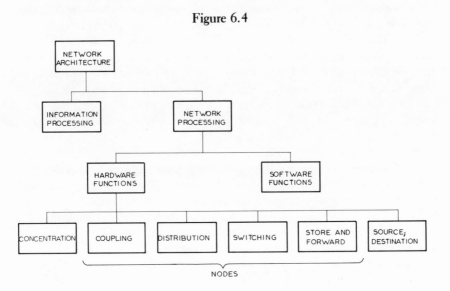

Figure 6.5

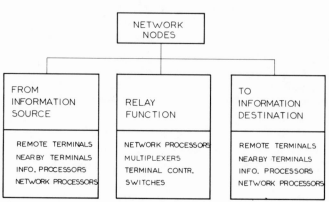

A protocol is balanced or symmetric when there is no master/slave relationship, that is, the network is horizontal. This is the new approach in networking, reflected in the X.25, LAP "B".*

A further definition necessary for a good understanding of how a network acts is that of the *topological layout*. This is an important prerequisite inasmuch as a topology is designed with specific objectives in mind. Protocols presuppose a given topology.† (There is *no* standard topology as such).

Projecting an Architecture

We said that within the framework of DIS, a architecture is a set of functions, interfaces, and protocols. Designing the architecture means to specify the functions that must exist at every node of a distributed information system. It also means projecting the interfaces between two functions of the same node. Usually functions interface through a protocol. This brings up the need for establishing or adopting protocols and for integrating them with the architectural framework. For instance, when we deal with programs which are able to exchange messages, we are faced with a *message protocol*. A *link protocol* is one whereby two functions exchange information on the physical lines, and so on.

Throughout the architectural perspective emphasis must be placed on long-term support of DIS developments, just as we appreciate the need for superior design and manufacture of computer products. This basic philosophy of a systems and a network architecture must be such that the user can rely on complete assistance to maintain the system at peak efficiency. A DIS must be backed by multiple resources, from efficient protocols to field service, training, and documentation. All important parts of a system must be subjected to highly detailed attention.

*Adopted in mid-1977 by the International Standards Organization. LAP stands for "line access protocol."

†Even if IBM's SNA and Digital Equipment's DECNET, etc., are more or less generalized.

Figure 6.6

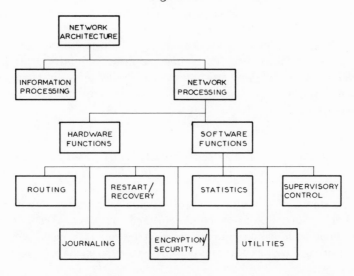

The architectural design must ensure, specification of requirements, reasonable cost, reliability and availability, and overall efficiency. The principles of design must be such as to enhance control action and to assess quality while it guarantees maintainability.

Complexity may be controlled through visibility—the process of making completely visible to project management all the constituents of the activities over which it is necessary to exercise direct control in time to promote systems simplicity.

Simplicity can be assessed by means of measurements—the need to measure, with great precision, progress toward well-defined design goals in terms of the observance of standards, the avoidance of intricate solutions, and the attention to established timescales and to performance criteria.

Simplicity helps quality. Mounting pressure to meet user needs, as expressed by the user and according to his own priorities, should not overshadow the requirement for quality results. Quality costs more, but in the final analysis offers the maximum benefit to all concerned.

Quality, in turn, promotes maintainability. The need to produce systems that have long useful lives, lower total life cycle costs, and sufficient flexibility to meet changing user demands is one of the indisputable basic facts in data communications.

Conclusion

The objective of an architecture for DIS is to provide an ensemble of instruments which permit the user to (1) proceed with an effective distribution of his hardware resources (device sharing); (2) put into action an optimal software distribution (program and procedure sharing); (3) effect the correct approach to a distributed data base network; (4) use high-level languages in approaching communications problems; (5) make full use of front-end and rear-end capability; (6) work in internetworking through the gateways; and (7) eventually implement distributed operating systems, on-line maintenance, encryption, security, and privacy. In order to competently help the user as far as the foregoing faculties are concerned, an architecture must be characterized by some specific capabilities inherent in its original design.

Device independence. The ability to utilize peripheral units of any type.

The ability to control remote peripherals as if they were local. Specifically, a program on remote computer or concentrator should be able to write directly into a disc of the higher level.

Program distribution. This characteristic permits the transmission of programs via a communication line to remote systems and subsequent execution. Such a faculty is important to remote equipment which does not have mass memory but is able to manage applications by means of requests posed to programs in other systems of the network.

Execution of system directives on remote equipment. This permits the activation or close down of programs between two remote computers, as well as downline loading and upline dumping.

Management of remote data bases. If the distributed system includes distributed data bases, it is necessary to provide for the management of a networkwide data base system. Such provision must account for the use of heterogeneous equipment.

The orderly approach to the design of the architecture would separate information processing from network processing, then integrate into a working ensemble the hardware and the software aspects. Figures 6.2 through 6.6 demonstrate this approach. The hardware and software functions are clearly distinguished. Each is crucial to the efficient and continuing performance of the network.

7

Functions and Objectives in Network Architecture

The architecture of data communication networks has evolved to a point where a common philosophy on functions and objectives is now emerging. The philosophy reflects a certain structure: the division of the networking functions into discrete modules and the layering of these modules such that higher layers or levels are built on the functions provided by the lower levels.

In order to structure the framework and to define the functions to be performed, it is advisable to divide a network architecture into communications, networking, and applications. Such layers are hierarchical, each one building on the abilities of the preceding or lower layers. The communication layer creates error-free sequential links from the physical channels connecting the network computers. The networking layer uses these links to route data from source to destination and create virtual circuits or Datagrams between the communicating programs or system resources. The application layer uses this communication path to control input–output devices, access files, and transmit application program data.

Most current network architecture use this layered structure. Within each of the layers a protocol is designed to perform the functions of that layer under the constraints and capabilities of the lower layers and physical equipment. This is the basis on which the concepts are developed. The network processing software, as it evolves, will necessarily reflect the design we have outlined.

Layered Solutions

One of the most important tests of a network architecture is that it is layered, and that the principle of independence between the layers is observed. This is fundamental since network architecture by its nature is a complex undertaking. The user needs layers and the concept of independence among layers to protect against

77

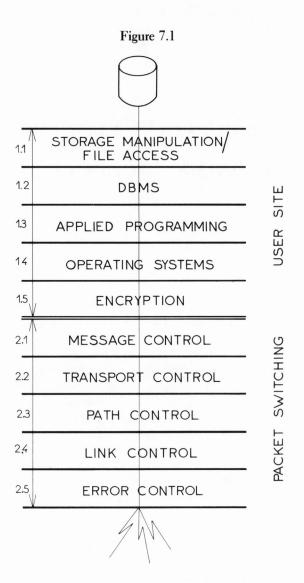

Figure 7.1

upheavals when changing successive functions or developing and inserting new ones.

We have distinguished information processing from network processing. The former is done at the user's site, while the latter is the object of packet switching. As Figure 7.1 demonstrates, each is divided into a number of subsets or constituent parts. For some of them, computer users already have well-established notions. Others, like encryption and path control, are still being developed.

At the user's site the overriding need is for terminal control. Assuming that in the future intelligent terminals will be commonplace, users will need to be assisted

Figure 7.2

SECTION	OBJECT
TRAILER	ERROR CONTROL
FRAME	LINK CONTROL
PACKET	PATH CONTROL
ID FRAGMENT	DTE OR CLUSTER CONTROLLER

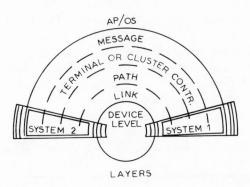

with DBHS and file access systems which would be available not just at a given central processing location but throughout the organization wherever a terminal exists. Record access protocols are necessary and these include user identification, file attributes, requests (open read; open write; delete), acknowledgments, data, and control functions.

At the applications level we must observe terminal access, network control, and remote system loading. Services to be provided within the packet-switching area will be overseen by the organization of the packet, which contains corresponding sections for each function to be performed; see Figure 7.2.

This explains how a layered solution helps two DTE (terminals or computer systems) communicate with each other. Within each layer, programs are written independently of the hardware reference, i.e., of the precise equipment which will be used.

We should also notice the role played by message control. The logical relation supported through the APs (applied programming) is independent from the physical relation of the nodes within which packet switching will be executed.

This leads to the idea of the maximum service a network architecture will provide; the network architecture offers the overall view on how the systems representation will be made. A logical organization, a physical organization, control and flow of information, and representation, interpretation and transformation of information—functions reflected since the original architectural design—are at the disposal of the user. The user's objective can thus be specified: to ensure that the faculties inherent to an architecture are used to their fullest extent.

Duties of the Network Architect

To make the network architect's job manageable, a sharp distinction must be made between architecture and implementation. The latter is the user's job. The network architect must confine himself scrupulously to (1) development of an overall concept, the definition of what it can do, and the examination of whether or not it answers the performance demanded; (2) evaluation of the project's ability to balance requirements with resources—putting the resources to work to the fullest extent; (3) spelling out the design specifications for further implementation; (4) testing needed to assure that the developing architecture respects the prerequisites in general and, in particular, the layered approach; (5) inclusion of standard protocols and the development of efficient interfaces; (6) making a comprehensive instruction text which is simple enough for less skilled people to use.

These are precise responsibilities to be performed step by step. Take, as an example, the functions of the networking layer: (1) *routing*—moving of data from source to destination; (2) *congestion control*—a global network problem; (3) *virtual channel management or Datagram solution*—inside this function we should distinguish: (a) *call establishment*, including message ACK, connection/disconnection, sequentiality, and flow control, and (b) *message segmentation*—the task of breaking messages into packets. Some of these functions will eventually be enhanced through international agreements, but this is not yet always the case. X.25, for example, still does *not* offer a true end-to-end ACK and flow control mechanism which means that either the network architect has to provide his own mechanism (hence, a minilayer), or accept the possibility of scrambling. The job is big, and it will necessarily have to be tackled by a team, which should be organized like a surgical team where one does the cutting and the others give him every support that will enhance his effectiveness.

The network architect and his team wili have to analyze the functions performed by level. Take the communications level as another example. Physical link, error detection, recovery, sequentiality (order in/out), and link management should all be examined. The last must ensure the mechanics of the operation: if there is more than one transmitter, there should be multiple control and ownership of the link by one transmitter at a time. Indeed, if we look at the interface to the communications layer, we see a *sequential* throughput: a multipoint link can be assimilated by many point-to-point hook-ups. These bring about the need for protocols. *If* there were many point-to-point connections—not a multidrop one—

Figure 7.3

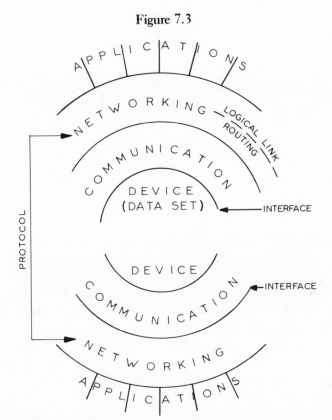

and *if* the total system were error free, we would not have needed the use of protocols for anything except framing.

Network architecture, however, does *not* really include the requirement of protocol design.* What it includes is the layers, the function definition *within* the layers, and the interface *between* the layers. These issues should attract the architect's attention.

Protocols and Interfacing

We have said that in order to handle its distributed data problems a network has to provide the solutions for interfacing (between layers) and protocols (between sender and receiver). Figure 7.3 demonstrates this relationship. The layers of communications and networking interface together. Within one layer there will be sublayers; for instance, link protocols break down into three functional components:

*In fact, it is better free of protocols so that protocols can be changed as new standards develop.

Figure 7.4

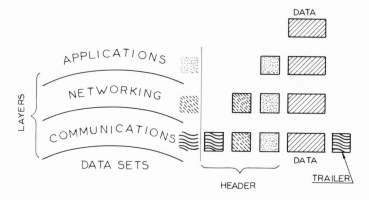

1. Framing—finding "beginning" and "end" of a message block
2. Data exchange—passing correct sequential data over the link
3. Link management—performing functions such as addressing receivers and selecting transmitters in the case of multiple transmitters and receivers

There follows the very important concept of "protocol purity." It means don't mix the protocols of the different layers, and don't use overlapping patterns. Figure 7.4 demonstrates how each layer adds to the packet its own reference. The header and the trailer are like brackets around the data. The header includes flags (mainly message priority), destination, and source. The trailer includes the control data.

Differences between protocols can exist all over, for example, in framing, where HDLC and SDLC versus DDCMP (digital data communication management protocol). The difference is in bit staffing even though both are synchronous disciplines. A need for special hardware results from the differences in question.

At the data exchange level, protocols are very similar regarding positive acknowledgment, retransmission and time-out occurrence. But they differ in efficiency.

Finally, the reference to link management concerns polling, tributary stations, contention, and symmetry. More precisely, it concerns whether there are primary/secondary solutions or whether all stations within the network are equal. Link management determines *when* a station sends a message, not *what* the station sends.

The Grand Design

Let us say that all problems relating to protocols and interfacing have been settled, and that the network architecture has been made to work efficiently and dependably. * What comes next? Let us assume that the network is a public service or, more

---

*Which might be a fact within four to five years.

Figure 7.5

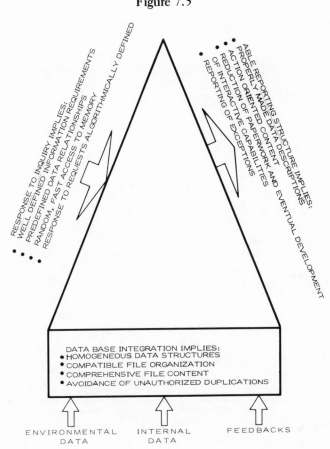

precisely, a value-added network. This is by far the most interesting development for a large number of industrial and commercial enterprises and financial institutions. The following, then, might be the grand design.

First, the availability of an efficient and dependable VAN would transfer to this Network most of the communications-related functions that are now performed by front ends, multiplexers, concentrators, and remote controllers. Among other functions, it would provide network control, flow control, code coversion, error control, terminal polling, message routing/rerouting and formatting.*

A high-level data communication language would allow the user to specify communications process requirements in standard form. Data, the most essential element in this new kind of system orientation, will become the center. The so-called arithmetic or central processor units will no longer be central—they will be auxiliary, away from the center or on the periphery of the system.

*In IBM terminology, the system would exclude access method (VTAM), but include network control program (NCP).

Figure 7.6

Equipment configuration. Today terminals are limited to 2,000 ft. direct connection; tomorrow, with optical fibers, to 7 miles. High-speed transmission minimizes core resource allocation and simplifies communications queueing. Control software at local sites is provided with minimum complexity.

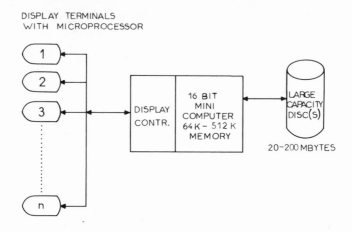

We emphasize these facts because they herald a different epoch in information system design and orientation. From a central processing unit-centered organization in 1950, we moved into a memory-centered system in 1965, and into a data-centered network in 1980. Organizations wishing to advance, not only keep up with but also profit from the evolution of technology, experience a major conceptual change. This is a 15-year cycle, and largely engulfs three generations of computers. Furthermore, the real growth of information systems will not be the amount of data—although this will grow substantially—but rather the use of that data. Control over data should be another prime subject of optimization.

The answer to the question of what to improve is that computer manufacturers should dedicate at least part of the greater processing engine power to providing easier, faster access to data, rather than using it merely as a means to house ever larger collections of data.

Another key function to optimize in systems to be delivered in the early 1980s concerns the format of the data whose access we seek to make more efficient. Still another refers to the data base management systems and their ability for ease of use, responsiveness, flexibility, and modularity. The input-output channels or their equivalent processors will also have increased data rates. Main storage will undoubtedly be substantially larger and faster with more functional designs, for example, hierarchical storage structures.

Both in business and, eventually, at home, the increasing business opportunity of information electronics will continue to displace other modes of control, reaching into nearly all aspects of our lives. The R + D money invested in this field will ensure that industry makes more sophisticated functional elements at ever decreasing costs. (These references are not made only in respect to data communications networks. Examples from everyday life abound. Mechanical elements of the calculator and the watch have been displaced by integrated circuits that are less expensive but more flexible. In the near future the automobile will be controlled by a microcomputer with a consequent improvement in efficiency.)

All these developments are extensions of the traditional application of electronics to the task of information handling in measurement, communication, and data manipulation. By the mid-1980s the number of electronic functions incorporated into existing products each year can be expected to be some fifty times greater than it is today. Correspondingly, the cost per function will decline by then to

Figure 7.7
Decentralized applications

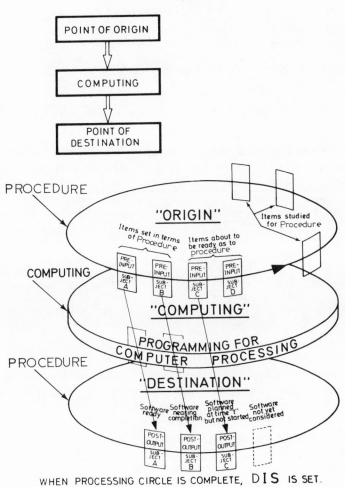

WHEN PROCESSING CIRCLE IS COMPLETE, DIS IS SET.

Table 7.1
The Two Main Resources at which the Systems Architecture Must Direct Attention

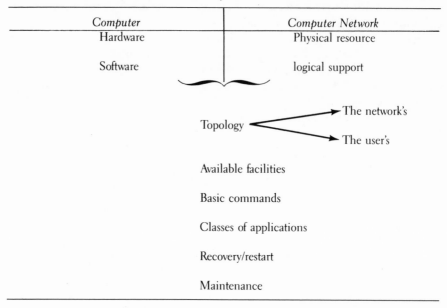

Computer	Computer Network
Hardware	Physical resource
Software	logical support

Topology → The network's
Topology → The user's

Available facilities

Basic commands

Classes of applications

Recovery/restart

Maintenance

between 1/15 and 1/20 of that of today, though in some areas where cost reduction during the last decade has been slow, the ratio might be much more impressive. Data communications is a specific case. As we stated earlier, with optical fibers, satellites, the multiplexing of voice, image, data, and the mass economies made possible through VAN, communications costs are projected to decrease by an impressive ratio, somewhere between 1/40 and 1/50 of where they stand today.

Impact at the Workplace

Developing an electronic mail service, expanding the data base and making its contents more accessible, providing interactive man-machine communications, disseminating knowledge for educational pruposes, and performing many of the clerical tasks in an office are tangible results to be expected from the exponential proliferation of products of data communications and of microelectronics.

The real evolution will be manifested in office routine. But how? An announcement made in late 1977 stated that the Firestone Tire and Rubber Co. was in the process of switching to a distributed processing system. The firm planned to split the data base and install both a terminal-based and a minicomputer-based system. Now we shall make the hypothesis that a VAN in operation was chosen to link the Firestone factories and sales offices, relieving the company from having to project its own network—as has been the case with Citinet. The decision to use

Table 7.2
The Potential of Networks

		Large systems > 10,000 terminals	Medium systems A. 1,000–10,000 B. 100–1,000 terminals	small systems A. 50–100 B. < 50 terminals
General Characteristics of use			1. Local 2. Telecommunications	COAX 700m Optical fibers 7km
Systems	Logical		Software	
functions	Physical		Hardware	

existing data communication facilities changes the perspectives of the study. The problem is dimensioned from network architecture to the level of a systems architecture, according to the distinction made in the preceding chapter.

With the network services taken care of, and provided that the user's analysts understand both the dynamics and the mechanics of data communications,* the salient problem of the user is that of the distributed data base. Over the last quarter of a century, the basic reason for the failures of computers was that the users were paying for big data processors but were only taking out of them the power of accounting machines. Let us not repeat the same failure with the networks.

Figure 7.5 brings this problem into focus: data base integration—*then* segmentation—response to inquiry, and able reporting structure are the three key issues. These will establish the requirements. The hardware study for the remote sites comes next. (And remember the rule for system architecture: dimension the equipment for the job to be done—not vice versa.)

The existence of VAN services may suggest the local use of intelligent terminals (see the discussion on the second and third generation of data communication networks in chapter 3). The equipment configuration may be as in Figure 7.6. The display units are equipped with a microprocessor and read-only memory and random-access memory. The use of intelligent terminals may allow connecting several of them into a small minicomputer 16-bit word and a 32-kiloword central memory. This system solution does *not* necessitate much buffering or complicated terminal switching techniques.

Relieved of the data communications chores which are delegated to the VAN, the local minicomputer can effectively act as a switch between the terminals and the data base. This solution requires that at the local site the terminals themselves

*Which, as we shall not fail to repeat, is a *key issue* and must always be kept in evidence. If one does not know data communications well, it is better not to work with the subject.

Table 7.3

	Physical System (+ basic logical system)	Logical (applications) System (MIS and client oriented)	Overall Network and Systems Maintenance
IT WAS	Hierarchial (asymmetric)	Hierarchical or Horizontal	Manual
NOW THE OBJECT IS	Symmetric	It must be a function of user requirements	Automatic (on-line) and Self-maintenance

queue-up the messages. In other words, the messages are *not* queued inside the computer but at the terminal level. A solution of this kind, incidentally, can just as well be used in a bank or in industry. With the new technologies where 16 kilobits and eventually 64 kilobits will be stored on a chip or two, a, say, 32-kilobyte memory is no obstacle. In fact, it's half a chip. The obstacle will be, as usual, the procedural study; see Figure 7.7. This is a known but rarely appreciated fact; we have to give it our most careful attention. Equipment is no real challenge today. The system architecture is.

Duties of the Systems Architect

In a given organization, the existing telecommunications skill, the age of the equipment, and the nature of the applications determine in a substantial part the general design performance and functional requirements for the new system—the more so as new systems and functional units require radical redesign of the old structures in order to give the best results.

Table 7.1 outlines the two main resources at which the systems architect must direct attention: computers and the computer network. He will deal with physical and logical supports, topology, applications, and systems functions. The potential of networks—their perspectives and facilities challenges—varies with the overall design, the number of terminals attached to them, the distance which must be covered, and the use to which they are put. This is shown in Table 7.2

Bank of America projects a network of 12,000 terminals; Montgomery Ward already has on-line some 19,000 terminals. There is a score of large important organizations in banking, transportation, manufacturing, merchandising—not to mention the governmental services—which think of upward of 10,000 terminals on-line.

Interflora, albeit a small organization by Bank of America or Montgomery Ward standards, has already over 1,000 terminals on Tymnet and plans for 3,000. There is an even bigger population of medium- and small-size companies thinking

Table 7.4

Architecture	
Network	*Systems*
	1. Effective Distribution of resources: A. *Hardware* Device sharing B. *Software* Process and program sharing
Rules must be established regarding device and program independence	
	2. Realization of a DDB
Establishment of a Networkwide DB/OS	
	3. Use of communications media and of communications languages
Design perspectives for perfect integration of media and languages	
	4. Linkage of user-oriented procedures and processes
	5. Use of different equipments and line disciplines
Study of project topology; programming and implementation	
	6. Host dependence or (better) independence
	7. Choice of protocols: *balanced *unbalanced
	8. Choice of switching methods: *circuit *message *packet

of terminals in the thousands. There is plenty of work for the systems architect without mixing with the network architect's job.

Table 7.3 makes the distinction among the physical system, the logical system, and the overall network and systems maintenance requirements. It pinpoints what the situation was and largely still is and what the objectives are now.

These objectives are better explained from the systems architect's viewpoint in Table 7.4. Several of the functions which are outlined interleave with the network architect's job. This is shown, but by and large what is written is the systems architect's responsibility. The systems architect will be applications oriented, using the network functions made available to him. He must understand these faculties and know how to put them to work, but he does not need to design them unless, as Citibank did, the organization designs its own data communications network.

8

The Trade-offs

Computers and data communications literature quite often fails to divide between network architecture and systems architecture. The difference is subtle but important. A network architecture is made up of a number of modular functions. Its goal is to simplify the task of description and implementation of a distributed environment, specifically one oriented to data communications. These functions may be implemented in hardware, software, or by human action. There will be a communications area—the backbone of the network—and a control area the network architect must provide for. These are not necessarily visible to the user. However, there is an applications area with which the user will interface; see Figure 8.1.

The general requirement of a network architecture is to provide networking capabilities across the broad range of functional uses. An architecture must be developed to support a wide variety of signal carriers, a broad range of processors, different operating systems, different data bases, and user interfaces. Because it is developed to operate within a transaction-oriented environment, the network architecture must ensure such supports on-line and through a complete interconnectability. This means supplying a mechanism where any pair of processes or devices can communicate.

The network architecture must use well-defined protocols and software facilities to achieve the desired ability to interconnect. It must also allow for future technological advances to be incorporated into the design and implementation with minimal upsetting of operations.

Trade-offs have to be made. Several of them relate to data representation. Will the communications system support only one data type or code? Two, three? What will be the format of the messages to be exchanged—fixed length and fixed fields? How much of a restriction will this be on the different applications to be handled on the network?

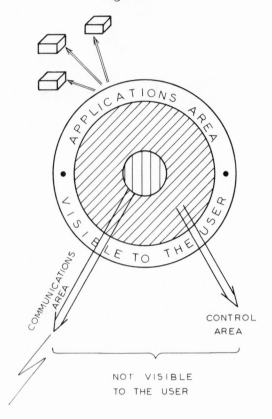

Figure 8.1

Trade-offs extend all the way into the applications domain. Should the communications system deliver the messages in a transparent manner, or should it provide a certain amount of data conversion? Of code conversion? Should it provide a certain amount of interpretation of the content of the messages, as electronic mail systems may require?

Which applications will be supported? Which hardware? Which software? Will services be provided to integrate existing hardware and software? Must the existing protocols be supported? What if the main current protocol is an old one that was designed for a limited application only?

Network Requirements

The line protocols to be supported and their impact on network control, network access, protection and security, response time considerations, error rates, and throughput are among the issues involved in a network planning study. Every factor to be studied involves trade-offs. Trade-offs among conflicting ends cannot be made intelligently unless the requirements have been established. Network requirements include:

1. Provision of a reasonably good network performance for each type of utilization
2. Assurance of a mechanism for connection to other networks
3. Support of functions necessary for protection and security
4. Assurance of correct accounting and billing procedures
5. Ease and efficiency in maintaining operations
6. High degree of availability

These are stated in generic terms; more specifically, the requirements will relate to the job. Do we wish to integrate voice, data, and image? Control the information and voice flow? Prepare statistics on the use of the system and on billing? Create network interfaces and gateways? In Figure 8.2, for instance, the circuit switching area is the telephone company's. The user has to think of PBXs and of terminals, of connection to the nearest port the backbone offers, and of cost and performance. And what about tomorrow—how will the unavoidable expansion be made?

The need for systems planning is evident. The network services will be developed over a number of years, but they must operate much longer. Continuous evaluation and maintenance are crucial issues for a successful life cycle. (Telenet has thirty men working on development with another thirty only on operations.) It is better to pay more capital cost in the beginning than a very high price during the whole life cycle.

One of the increasingly significant problems facing the designers and planners is the timely and accurate definition of systems elements, activity interrelationships, and their interfaces. A specific issue within a network environment is "sockets." The

Figure 8.2

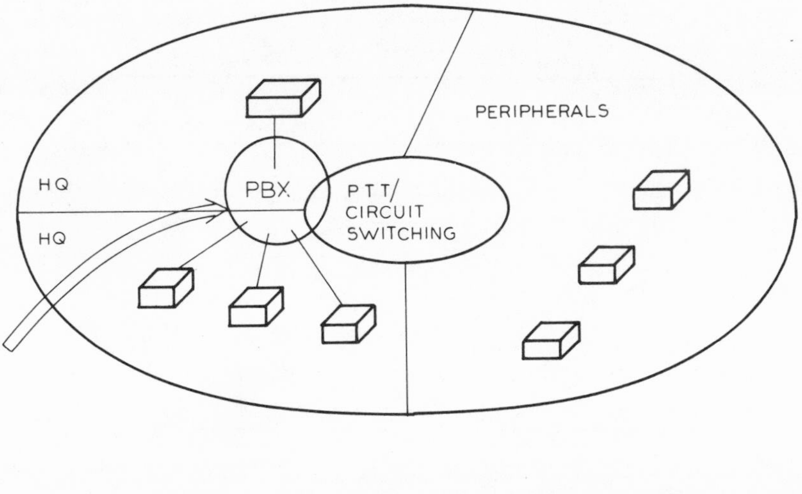

definition of sockets is important in process-to-process communications and connection procedures, both establishment and rejection; see Figure 8.3.

Assume that processes have input–output ports whose names are peculiar to operating system implementation. Processes themselves may be identified in different ways in various operating systems. Imagine that the host-to-host protocol must provide a uniform name space so that a process in one system can effectively "connect" a local port to a remote one by reference to the common naming conventions. Assume that the common naming conventions will be translated into local conventions by the host-to-host protocol program. We will refer to the implementation of a host-to-host protocol as a control program, (CP). The common names for ports will be sockets and these will implicitly identify the host and process

Figure 8.3

This multilayered structure is necessary to ensure that data do not get lost. The ports are defined locally and are idiosyncratic. The socket reflects a uniform, standard name space.

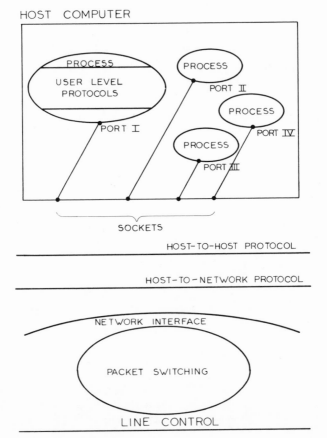

Figure 8.4

Criteria for choosing networks: error protection, available protocols, gateways to other networks, speed of transmission, store facilities, parametrically defined functions

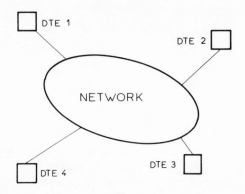

owning the port. A process can range between COBOL (or any language) program, a library, a file system, a whole data base, a peripherals handler (e.g., printer) and its software, and a rear-end machine.

Processes need both hardware and software resources to be run and sockets through which to communicate with their environment. In a remote communications network, the communicating objects are typically terminals and processes—the latter usually being unaware of the physical location of the former. Indeed, the location of the device, file, or program is usually unimportant as long as it is accessible. As far as the user is concerned, the location is determined by the functions which are performed, while accessibility is assured by the network.

The Seven Basic Steps

Lack of internal expertise in many companies creates the situation where they are asking for a network for data communications without specifying whether the need is for inquiry–response, interactive problem solving, transaction-oriented requirements, bulk data transfer, or other possibilities. Alternative solutions, for example, facsimile, could answer the needs. These alternatives have very different kinds of requirements in terms of the parameters of choice.

As Figure 8.4 demonstrates, criteria exist for choosing networks, and these are largely user oriented. Choices have to be made. To satisfy user-oriented requirements—both current and future—many techniques may be employed which center around the structure and the protocols.

The first technique is *layering and modularization*. The functions to be performed by the network architecture may be divided into modules and structured in a layered manner. We shall talk of layers in the following section. Here, it is

Figure 8.5
A total mechanism showing a network with different levels of transmission speeds and usage

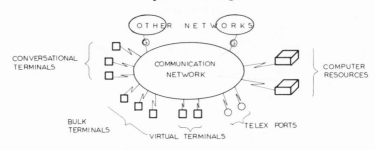

· TERMINAL-TO-TERMINAL	· AUTOMATIC TERMINAL RE-COGNITION	· ERROR DETECTION AND CORRECTION
· TERMINAL-TO-COMPUTER	· HOST AVAILABILITY	· STORE AND FORWARD
· TERMINAL EMULATION	· TERMINAL/HOST ROUTING	· ALTERNATE PATH SELECTION
· INTERACTIVE AND BULK TERMINALS	· PROTECTION/PRIVACY	· NETWORK RELIABILITY

sufficient to remark that high-level layers use the functions provided by lower layers in a strictly hierarchical ordering. This creates a flexible architecture and ensures efficient implementation. It has, however, a cost, namely, interfacing (between layers) and implementation overhead.

Architectural design and subsequent implementation may structure each layer as a separate task or process, provide the communications link between them, or combine several layers into a single process (using subroutine calls to pass information and control). The implementation must make use of the logical solutions available within the system. Hence, an architectural design must project and provide from the beginning for such techniques.

Always keep in mind that trade-offs extend into all three areas of a network: the physical (nodes, communications links), the logical (rules, commands), and that of the subscriber (to use the physical facilities, these subscribers must observe the logical constraints). From among the conflicting requirements the designer faces, he must strike the right balance.

A second technique, *layered abstraction*, is a basic characteristic of layered solutions. A level of abstraction is created by each layer in the structure to the layer above it. A simpler way of saying this is that functions (and sometimes structure) specific to a given layer are used within that layer; they are not passed to layers above. A lower layer, for instance, manages the data link control. Such functional characteristics are transparent to the next level which manages the routing function. In turn, this is transparent to the next level which addresses itself to virtual circuit service.

The functional mechanism technique follows the overall design and also complements it. Such a mechanism must ensure that functions specific to a given application or use of the system are, as far as possible, moved to the user level; additions, deletions, or changes in specific uses do not affect the networking portion of the architecture; any function can be moved to a higher level without affecting the complexity of the interfaces or the basic structure.

Because we are still at the early stages of architectural developments, we should avoid making systems rigid. Today security protection, and the information required, may be handled by the same layer. Tomorrow one layer might provide the information necessary for security and protection, but the mechanism proper could be the object of a higher layer.

Figure 8.5 shows a total mechanism. It lists functions whose objective is to provide a network with the broadest appeal to the user. Therefore, different levels of transmission speeds and use have been incorporated.

In the *protocols within protocols* technique not only are the network functions layered, but the corresponding protocols are structured one inside the other. This is known as nesting of protocols. Each functional layer should look at the protocol envelope which concerns it directly and should not involve the other protocol layers. This approach—handling protocols only at the architectural layer to which they correspond—gives the flexibility to add or subtract new protocols.

The *layers within layers* technique designs the layers of a network architecture and the corresponding protocols with sublayers (or subsets). This ensures flexibility in future expansion or upkeep. To some extent it also makes feasible that part of the whole system might adhere to the structure of another architecture. Indeed, this is the course new architectures have followed. Table 8.1 documents this by comparing the layered approach of three architectures: Digital Equipment Corporation's Decnet, Hewlett-Packard's 3000, and IBM's SNA. This table also presents the terminology used by each of the three manufacturers—notice that it is not standard—and, correspondingly, the terminology the reader will find in this book.

In the *resources and their use* technique reference is made to system resources and functional modules for communication and identification. This can be done using a global "object type" descriptor, mapped locally into the process to which communication is addressed. It is necessary to ensure that each system, subsystem, and process knows about its local characteristics—whether or not it is needed to pass this information to other parts of the network.

Let us recall what was said of processes and sockets. Figure 8.6 shows a multiprogrammed maxicomputer operating in a typical banking environment. This is a resource at the user's level, but at the network level it is a data load. Serving equipment calls for resources and requires interfaces. A computer gateway needs to be provided.

A final technique is to take a *long hard look* at the network architecture. It must be designed so all nodes operate within a given structure. The functional use of a node depends on its physical location in the network and the user-oriented functions it is designed to perform. The architecture treats nodes either as switches or as local intelligence. The latter may be hosts, front ends, terminal concentrators, or terminals and will be handled identically from a network perspective.

There will be many design issues to consider. One of the most important is that of the trade-offs, for instance, between line efficiency and processing optimization. Further, the design of a network architecture for general-purpose networks must

Table 8.1

Common Carriers (CCITT* recommendation X.25)	Decnet (Digital Equipment Corporation)	3000 (Hewlett-Packard)	SNA (IBM)	Corresponding Terminology used in this book
Users' level: referred to as level 4	Dialogue layer	User protocol / User interface / Host services	Function management	Users' layer, divided into several distinct levels
Level 3	Network services protocol (NSP layer)	Distributed system monitor / Network system	Transmission control / Path control	Networking/virtual circuit or datagram / Networking/routing
Level 2	DDCMP (digital data communication management protocol)	Protocol driver (communication)	SDLC	XDLC communications layer (data link control, link management)
Level 1	—	—	—	DCE / DTE

*International Telephone and Telegraph Consultative Committee

Figure 8.6

Multiprogrammed maxicomputer operating in a banking environment

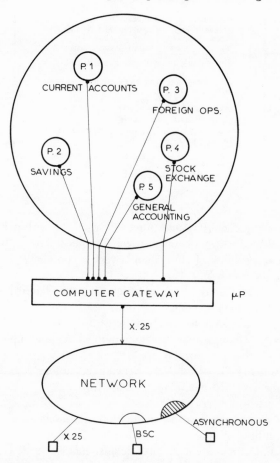

account for the variety in the kinds of messages to be transmitted. An effort should, therefore, be made from the start to accommodate large as well as small messages in the most efficient manner. Tymnet, for instance, worked on this solution.

Finally, with internetworking it will be necessary to have a multiaddress scheme. Small networks use a single-part address, while larger ones can expand into multipart addresses. One way is to make addressing hierarchical.

Layered Communications Principles

Protocols and processes may be layered and ordered so that the higher level assumes that the functions provided by the lower level exist and are ensured in an able manner.

Figure 8.7

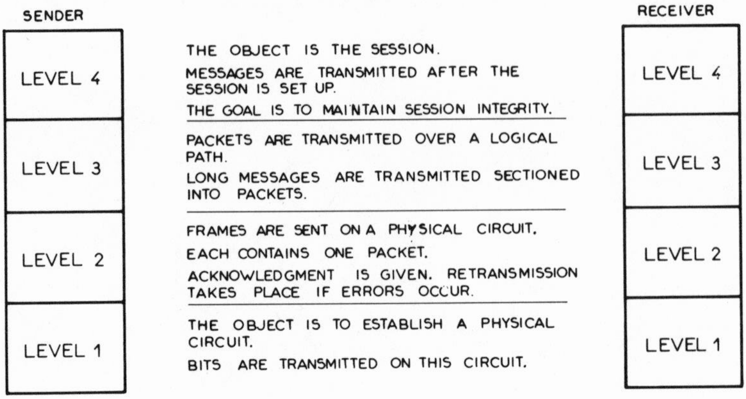

SENDER		RECEIVER
LEVEL 4	THE OBJECT IS THE SESSION. MESSAGES ARE TRANSMITTED AFTER THE SESSION IS SET UP. THE GOAL IS TO MAINTAIN SESSION INTEGRITY.	LEVEL 4
LEVEL 3	PACKETS ARE TRANSMITTED OVER A LOGICAL PATH. LONG MESSAGES ARE TRANSMITTED SECTIONED INTO PACKETS.	LEVEL 3
LEVEL 2	FRAMES ARE SENT ON A PHYSICAL CIRCUIT. EACH CONTAINS ONE PACKET. ACKNOWLEDGMENT IS GIVEN. RETRANSMISSION TAKES PLACE IF ERRORS OCCUR.	LEVEL 2
LEVEL 1	THE OBJECT IS TO ESTABLISH A PHYSICAL CIRCUIT. BITS ARE TRANSMITTED ON THIS CIRCUIT.	LEVEL 1

The architecture centers around functions which are well defined within the layer, and if redefined will not necessarily touch other layers.

The interchangeability of component layers is considered in terms of functionality within the network.

Specific implementations of the architecture may be tailored.

Internetworking interfaces may be more easily provided since only some components need translation to the client network's code.

Future design changes may be implemented without upsetting the total structure or the unchanged portions.

Further layers may be added as the network technology develops, particularly layers at the user level where developments are still weak.

Figure 8.7 presents the now classic division into layers for a packet-switching network. It identifies both the object and the functions.

Several technical requirements must be answered to ensure layered solutions. Layered communications involve a clear definition and separation of tasks, the dedication of a layer to each major task (data link, routing, and so on), the ability of adjacent layers to communicate via interfaces and of equivalent layers to communicate via protocols.

Protocols and interfaces must be supported by a sound software (or firmware). These reside in each processor in the network, or, if distributed, they are accessible by each processor as the need arises.

Each layer must answer the prerequisites of a communication mechanism. This involves both the processing of data and the control of the communication system and its components.

Components of communications systems are the devices and their software, conversation establishment, the routing of messages, flow control, error detection, and so on. Every one of these components serves the purpose of the network

Figure 8.8

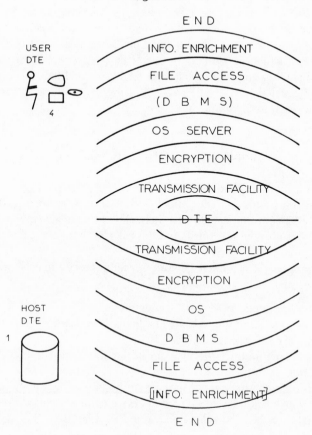

architecture, namely, the transfer of data between applications or processes, operating on different systems using data links between the systems supporting the processes. Emphasis is on the processes, and it is in this regard that the end-to-end reference should be made; see Figure 8.8.

The data being transferred may be a single character, an entire file, a program to be executed, or an entire library. The DTE (terminal, hosts) used in the network may be of different families, with a variety of operating systems, using different data types and structures. The links between systems may be permanent and stable or temporary (dial-up). They may be of different speeds, synchronous or asynchronous, and use a variety of protocols.

Whatever solution is chosen it should not alter the way the user communicates at a high-level protocol. Between the bit-level data access and the user's dialogue there is room for many layers of protocols.

Let us recapitulate. The layered communications concept must be supported end-to-end in a topologically independent way. At all times, the communications mechanism must allow objects (DTE, processes) to carry on a dialogue. The processes must agree to conduct the dialogue by undergoing a connection (session establishment) procedure though they may not perform a direct object-to-object communication, which is particularly true of devices. The general communications mechanism thus consists of three parts: establish, conduct, and disconnect the process-to-process dialogue. Each layer within the communications system has a role to play in each of these functions.

Implementing a Layered Solution

The communications mechanism ensures data exchange between processes residing in the system. Programs, data files, input–output devices, and terminals exchange information over communications channels. The functional requirements of the communications must be supported, and this calls for both physical and for logical resources.

These components of a layered communications process may be divided in the following way, starting from the lower level:

1.   Hardware interfaces (data set, modem DCE)
2.   Communications (physical link particularly concerned with call establishment, data integrity, and control)
3.   Networking/routing (the prerequisite for the logical link layer, dialogue control)
4.   Networking/virtual circuit or datagram (establishing the logical link)
5.   User/application level (oriented to device control, applications, data base) which may be subdivided into a number of layers

As figures 8.7 and 8.8 also demonstrated, in an end-to-end solution the first layer is concerned with physically moving digital information from one geographical location to another. It may include (and most likely will) equipment from different manufacturers: modems, interfaces, and lines.

The second layer guarantees the basic parts of a communications mechanism: data link establishment and link control. Among it functions are specific dialogue faculties such as error control. This layer takes care of the maintenance of data integrity and sequencing across a signal carrier which connects two or more processors and/or devices. Correcting errors typically introduced by signal carriers, and the addressability of DTE are also handled by this layer.

The third layer controls the flow of information, guarantees sequential data delivery within the network, and controls end-to-end communication. It is also concerned with the location of services, the guarantee that a topologically connected network is virtually connected, and the optimality of the paths that messages take through the network—in brief, the routing component.

Figure 8.9

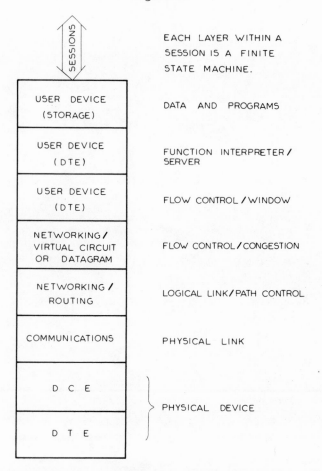

The fourth layer addresses itself to provision of generic services obtainable in the network. They include a user (application) program, a task or process loader, a file system, a printing device, an operator's console, and so on.

Figure 8.9 shows three user layers prior to reaching the objective establishing a session. Each performs a distinct set of functions and presents a level of abstraction to the higher layer. Such functions and their implementation are reflected in a protocol.

9
Switching: Circuit, Message, and Packet

This chapter digresses from the coverage of network architecture and looks more closely into the PTT/AT&T area of lines and switches identified in the preceding chapter (see Figure 8.2).

The discussion of trade-offs has not yet ended. Indeed, one of the biggest issues is the choice of switching technology. Let us look at the fundamentals. Switching choices essentially mean a decision on how to share the communications facility. With point-to-point operations the alternatives are multiplexing and switching. With multipoint (broadcast, multidrop) approaches we have a choice between polling and contention. They all involve line switching. There are three basic switching disciplines available for line switching: circuit, message, and packet.

Circuit switching is the oldest and the most used. This classic approach provides a "total path." There is a setup time for call establishment; call termination results in the circuit being dropped. Circuit switching may have many different aspects and offer a variety of service levels.

With message switching, one user talks to the other while a record is kept, for instance, on disc. The message can be controlled for errors. Other services are offered, such as store and forward. Hence, while with circuit switching one user talks directly to the other, with message switching all messages transmit via a processor (for instance, minicomputer) which registers prior to transmitting. This has opened up extensive possibilities, since the minicomputer can link to other minicomputers with different protocols, elaborate the text it receives, check for "passwords," and provide inquiry capabilities, to mention only a few services.

Packet switching is a newer, more elaborate form of message switching.* It presupposes data transmitted in discrete quantities. Messages are created as individual blocks or packets which "hop" from node to node. The transmission

---

*This statement can be controversial. Not everyone accepts it. But we shall see the reason for it in the more detailed discussion which follows.

Figure 9.1

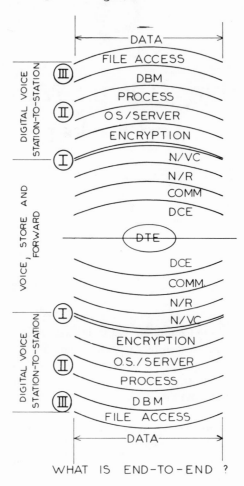

WHAT IS END-TO-END ?

facilities are shared all the time. A packet is a unit of information with predefined length. Its very special characteristic is that it is *not* oriented to a specific application. To the contrary, message switching *is* oriented to the application. This is a basic characteristic to which several references will be made.

Notice that all three methods allow resource sharing which is fundamental to any data communications system. And all three methods accept data and voice communications capabilities; see Figure 9.1. Data and voice can coexist up to a point—the logical path. This opens tremendous horizons for voice communications since it makes available store and forward capabilities. With this perspective there are three levels of an end-to-end reference the reader must follow (identified as I, II, and III in the figure).

The problem to which the following sections are addressed is this: Given the

Figure 9.2
Circuit switching (S = sender; D = destination; A and B are nodes over which messages travel)

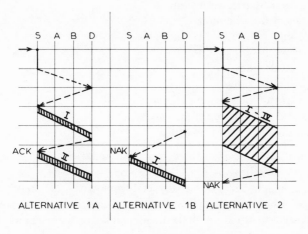

possibilities of alternatives, what are the relative strengths and weaknesses of each method?

Circuit Switching

The best example of circuit switching is the dial telephone network. The user dials the desired number. The network switches assign a circuit from source to destination, but the lines may be busy and delays result in setup. If answered, the circuit is established. In multipoint, a primary station authorizes a secondary station to transmit—thus assigning a circuit. This circuit remains assigned to the call until the call is terminated. During the communication time, the circuit is dedicated to this particular operation, whether or not data is transmitted.

The basic characteristics of circuit switching may be outlined as follows: First, it involves the establishment of a total path at all initiations. This results in significant inflexibility, given the way in which current voice-grade networks are implemented. Second, the circuit is established by a special signaling message which threads its way through different switching centers. Third, this circuit (being a total path) is subject to the speed and code limitations of the slowest link. As stated, the total path remains allocated for the transmission, regardless of utilization. Call termination results in the circuit being dropped, each line and switch returning to a pool of available circuits. Figure 9.2 is an example of circuit-switching data transmission.

Circuit switching has three advantages:

1. Circuit routing is simpler.
2. The discipline is the most widespread today.

3.   There is the possibility to attach terminals with different characteristics.

There are, however, many disadvantages:

1.   No automatic retransmission
2.   Inefficient use of circuits
3.   Switching failures fatal to the traffic
4.   Inefficient to "bursty"* traffic
5.   Voice-grade lines
6.   No record-keeping
7.   Long setup time (with traditional circuits)
8.   No speed- or code-matching capability
9.   Relatively high error probability

Errors filter through since there is no particular preoccupation with error control in circuit switching.

It must be emphasized that many of the problems of circuit switching—connect times, bandwidth, conditioning, voice and data imcompatibility—are common to current networks. With the new technologies the entire way of handling communications traffic will change—and circuit switching will be able to stage a comeback. Intelligent terminals will be doing speed change, buffering, editing, and the like. Use can then be made of circuit switching's relative advantages over other network solutions: its widespread acceptance† and the fact that circuit switching can handle traffic *without* preallocating resources. With other methods, for instance, store and forward, this cannot be done.

We may use a circuit (and the circuit-switching discipline) to connect two stations, T1 and T2—and only these two stations (Figure 9.3). This is known as point-to-point. It has been used in the past and is still used extensively, but it is an inefficient solution for long distances and large networks. When terminals do not transmit to the central computer (or through the central resource to each other), the line is idle—and lines are expensive.

An improvement would be to put more terminals on the same line, but now we run into addressing problems. We have to solve them and program our solutions. Or, we may adopt network approaches, and let the network do the job. This is what packet switching, for instance, does.

Let us repeat what we have said. If point-to-point communications media are chosen, the system may be organized at the host level around multiplexing or switching. However, if multipoint (multidrop or broadcast) is used, polling and contention are two alternatives for resource sharing.

In *contention*, communication can be initiated by either the terminal or the computer, if there are messages to be sent to the computer and vice versa. Either can start up transmission sending a signal to the other to reserve the line. A typical contention procedure carries out the following phases: the unit, ready to operate, asks for the go-ahead to transmit; the receiving unit gives the go-ahead; the

---

*For example, when many devices enter the circuit at the same time.
†17,000 exchanges in the United States alone don't need to change.

Figure 9.3

POINT–TO–POINT/OWN LINE, ONE SOLUTION

T1 O————————————————O T2

SWITCHING CENTERS/ MANY SOLUTIONS

- POINT–TO–POINT
- MULTIDROP/DEDICATED LINE
- MULTIDROP/FIRST PRIORITY
- DATA NETWORK

ALSO MANY TECHNOLOGIES
1. SPACE DIVISION
2. FREQUENCY DIVISION
3. TIME DIVISION

NETWORK APPROACHES/ ONE SOLUTION

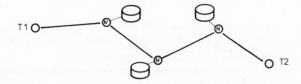

transmitting unit starts transmission; the receiving unit signals correct message reception; the transmitting unit closes down the transmission process.

In a contention system each subscriber attempts to communicate information to a central computer. This takes place at the time the information becomes available or at a locally determined time soon thereafter. Stated differently, systems transmit whenever they wish and resolve collisions of two systems transmitting simultaneously by means of variable delays and retransmission. This procedure can jeopardize the behavior of the two units in the following cases: (a) the receiving unit does not give the go-ahead for transmission; (b) the transmitting unit does not receive the transmission go-ahead within a certain time limit; (c) the receiving unit signals that the message has been received incorrectly, but the transmitting unit does not receive the signal; (d) the characters for message reception do not reach the transmitting unit.

Additional features, such as carrier detect, may be added to reduce the collision problem. (As with any scheme, times are necessary to recover from outages. Link management information may be lost and recovery action is necessary.)

Figure 9.4
Polling

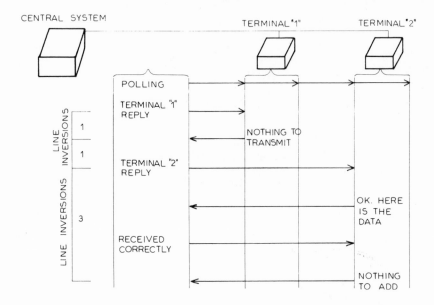

Contention has, however, many advantages. One of them is not using the computer's resources, when there is no traffic present; because of this it is used by several networks, Ethernet and Alchanet being examples.

Polling is a technique for controlling the use of lines by agreed protocols between devices trying to share a common transmission path; see Figure 9.4. By means of polling, the user places the terminals in a "speak only when spoken to" mode (as contrasted to contention). While all terminals will sense a given poll, only one will respond to it. The terminals must be rigidly controlled, given that all of them use the same principal line.

There are two types of polling disciplines in common use: roll call (or bus) and hub (or distributed).

Roll call polling is governed by the central computer which sends a control message to each terminal in turn, inviting it to transmit a message. The terminal replies either with transmit message, or with a control message indicating that it has nothing to report. One system—the control—polls or invites tributary systems to transmit, maintaining central orderly control of the link. Polling carried out in this way obtains reasonable flexibility because the computer may recognize the order of polling should it become necessary. On the other hand, a high proportion of control messages have to pass through the network and this tends to make it inefficient. Furthermore, among the disadvantages is the delay resulting from the large number of line inversions; see Figure 9.5.

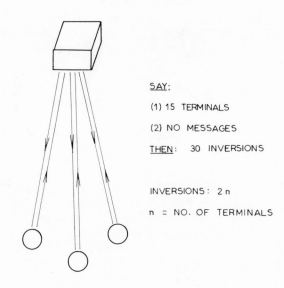

SAY:

(1) 15 TERMINALS

(2) NO MESSAGES

THEN: 30 INVERSIONS

INVERSIONS: 2 n

n = NO. OF TERMINALS

In hub polling the control system creates a poll command, which is then passed along the path of a multipoint circuit. The computer invites the first terminal to send a message; if none is ready, the first terminal passes the request to the second terminal and so on. This is particularly efficient when the terminals are inactive and lines are very long; see Figure 9.6. Whenever a terminal replies with an information message, the computer deals with it, and then resumes the polling sequence by inviting the next terminal to proceed. In this way an active terminal near the beginning of the circuit is prevented from monopolizing the attention of the computer. At the completion of the cycle—with all resources connected into the loop interrogated—the host regains control.

Another technique of polling when concentrators are used is to allow each remote concentrator to poll the terminals connected to it. This is more efficient than polling from the central computer because each multiplexer operates in parallel and there are fewer control messages involving the computer itself.

Polling is typical of party-line configurations, but may also be employed in point-to-point. Several types of messages may exist, however. A terminal may reply "failure" to the control characters which authorize transmission. Faulty message reception sent by the terminal or central system may call for repetition. Reception failure on the part of the terminal (or central system) of the control characters sent by the central system (or terminal) will initiate a whole error routine.

Selecting is employed for the transfer of messages from the central system to the terminals or other remote devices. As such, it forms an integral part of a polling and

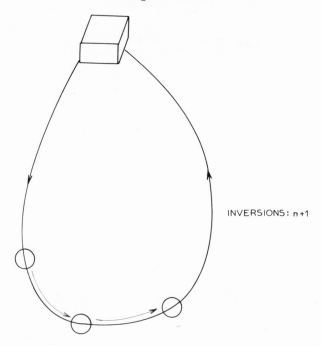

INVERSIONS: n+1

selecting procedure. In polling and selecting, whether transmission comes from terminal to computer or vice versa, it is always the computer which puts the proceedings into motion.

Message Switching

Message switching developed from the tape systems originally used for telegraphic switching and Telex. Figure 9.7 gives an example of a message-switching application. This method is also known as "traffic dispatcher" and "message router." With message switching, the messages are small—64 to 256 bytes—and are not decomposed into small elements by the network because they are oriented to the application.

The contrast to circuit switching is interesting. While with circuit switching one user talks directly to the other, with message switching all messages transmit via the central unit (minicomputer) which registers the messages prior to transmitting. Furthermore, the minicomputer can:

Figure 9.7

Message switching (S = sender; D = destination; A and B are nodes over which messages travel)

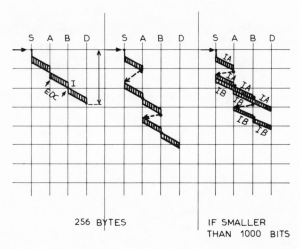

1.   Link to other minicomputers with different protocols
2.   Elaborate the text it receives
3.   Check for "passwords"
4.   Provide inquiry
5.   Handle multiaddress traffic
6.   Distinguish priority traffic
7.   Provide for error control and recovery
8.   Allow code conversion as the subscriber passes messages to a subnetwork, which accepts messages from or sends messages to distant terminals
9.   Analyze headers for destination, special processing, etc.
10. Take responsibility for delivery

In brief, with message switching one user talks to the other but there is a record kept, e.g., on disc, and the message can be controlled for errors. Message switching will *not* pass the message to the terminal until it is assured that it is complete and error free. This may result in delays since messages are not decomposed into smaller elements.

Store-and-forward techniques—originally developed for message switching—provide greater throughput. Indeed, the emphasis of a switching application is on fast transmission (as in the case of packet switching) or greater throughput. Store and forward may include peripheral storage systems such as magnetic discs or drums. It is useful with link protocol conversion, code conversions, message monitoring, message recording, etc. Buffer and queue delays frequently are long so that interactive delay requirements cannot be met.

Figure 9.8

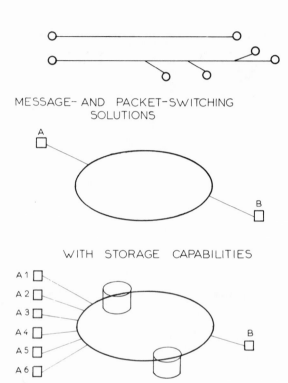

RIGID CONNECTIONS

MESSAGE- AND PACKET-SWITCHING
SOLUTIONS

WITH STORAGE CAPABILITIES

The impact of storage capabilities is shown in Figure 9.8. The old, rigid connection has ceased to exist, and points A and B communicate through the network facilities. Adding storage capabilities at the nodes disassociates A from B. Now many A's can communicate over the same line—without B feeling this multiplex—for any practical purpose.

Store and forward messages are typically terminal to terminal or unsolicited host output messages stored on disc and routed to the destination. They involve a wider variety of destinations than core-switched traffic and require more extensive routing capabilities.

For core-switched traffic, routing functions are necessary: extraction of the destination logical identifier, determination of the destination line and station tables, completion of the control block for output with the appropriate routing data, and queuing the control block for output.

Similar functions are necessary for disc-switched traffic: edit: extract the routing data from the message content; route: use the routing data to determine the logical identifier and then the line and station tables; tag build: complete the control block

Figure 9.9

Packet switching. The message is divided into three packets of nominal size;
each travels independently to destination.

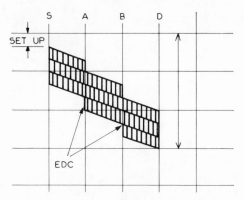

and build additional control blocks as required for multiple deliveries; queue: queue the control blocks, send message acknowledgments, and write logs as necessary.

A typical queueing program writes the control blocks to the appropriate output queues in disc. It also updates the queue pointers retained in core, sends acknowledgments when required, sets the flag for output service action, and may perform logging. A typical output queue service program reads the control block entries from disc queues, reads the message segments from disc, and interfaces with the appropriate input–output routine to initiate output.

Store and forward permits a tremendous capability applicable not only to data transmission but also to voice and image. Briefly stated, the sender and the receiver are decoupled. No longer is there a one-to-one correspondence of the wire circuit type or its equivalent.

Two, three, or n senders may be hooked up on the same node, same physical facility transmitting messages through time-division multiplexing (TDM). The messages (more precisely, their parts) are stored, then forwarded, in the most efficient way the network permits at speeds which made this process hardly noticeable or, more often, not noticeable at all.

Packet Switching

Packet switching is a block of data organized for transmission with both a minimum and a maximum length and which obeys packet protocol rules. It had its origin in message switching, but it is not applications oriented. A record or message longer than the maximum must be split into submessages. The maximum is 1,000 to 2,000 or up 8,000 bits. If the message is longer, it is divided into packets of nominal size and each travels independently to its destination; see Figure 9.9.

Table 9.1

Comparison of Three Disciplines

Circuit Switching	Message Switching	Packet Switching
1. Uses classical electromechanical (or computerized) switching centers	Fairly intelligent message-switching center is needed, with storage facilities	Switching computers used at the nodes; can be micromini, mini, or midi
2. A wire circuit (or its equivalent radio link) connects the parties	No direct wire connection	No direct wire connection
3. Point-to-point transmission	Permits broadcast and multi-address of messages	Permits broadcast and multiaddress of messages
4. Transmission is fixed bandwidth on voice-grade lines	Usually low-speed transmission (sub-voice)	Users effectively employ small or large bandwidth according to need
5. Network cannot perform speed or code conversion	Network can perform speed or code conversion	Network can perform speed or code conversion
6. No delayed delivery possible	Delayed delivery is feasible if the recipient is not available or the lines are busy	Delayed delivery is possible as a special network facility
7. Network and its facilities are of a generalized type	Network and its facilities are applications oriented	Network and its facilities are of a generalized type
8. No particular optimization of speed of transmission or throughput	Optimization is made in terms of throughput	Optimization is primarily for speed of transmission
9. No store and forward	Store-and-forward capability	Store and forward is possible
10. Switched path is established for the entire conversation	Route is originated for each message	Route is established dynamically for each packet

11. Time delay in setting up the call	Call setup is reasonable	Negligible delay in setting up the call; usually the least of the three alternatives
12. Negligible transmission delay	Delay in message delivery can be substantial	Negligible delay in packet delivery
13. Busy signal if called party is occupied	No busy signal. Store and forward solution	Packet returned to sender if undeliverable
14. Increased probability of blocking because of overload	Increased delivery delay because of overload	Overload results in increased delivery delay, but delivery time is short
15. NO effect on transmission once the connection is made	Saturation has a great impact on delay	Blocking when saturation is reached
16. Old type of real time between the parties.	Too slow for conversational interaction	Old type of real time unnecessary since conversational interaction is assured through modern technology
17. Messages are not filed at the nodes	Messages can be filed at the nodes	Messages are not filed, except for journaling purposes
18. Protection against loss of messages is the responsibility of the end user	Protection against loss of messages is responsibility of the network	Protection against loss of packets is responsibility of network with virtual circuits, of user with datagrams
19. Any length of transmission is permitted	Lengthy messages can be transmitted directly	Lengthy messages are divided into packets (1,000 to 8,000 bits each)
20. Economical with low traffic volumes, if public lines are employed, but very expensive with private lines	Economical with moderate traffic volumes	Reasonably high traffic volumes needed for economic justification but less expensive than private lines

Packet switching transmits data in discrete quantities. Messages are created as individual packets or groups of packets (i.e., decomposed into small elements by the network) which "hop" from node to node. Transmission facilities are shared all the time. There is no prerequisite of secondary storage (the original packet switching could also be seen as message switching without secondary storage). Packets are routed independently (pipelining), and message delay is typically a fraction of a second. Systems allow for effective use of circuit bandwidth and of intelligent switches. The network establishes the responsibility for queuing the messages in the right sequence.

This requires powerful minicomputers and more storage (disc) capacity at the nodes. In the late sixties and early seventies minicomputers were marketed at low prices and offered a high cost/performance ratio, making packet switching economically feasible. The price made it more economical to assign dynamically costly transmission capacity by the packet than to preassign a fixed bandwidth (end-to-end) subchannel to each call or session.

Packet switching is characterized by the routing of data through a network in discrete quantities at bit transmission level. Each packet includes a header, information, and a trailer. Messages are created as individual packets or groups of packets, within the specified limits. Packets, in transit at all times, "hop" from node to node. They are error checked, queued, routed, and stored and forwarded. Packet switching provides line and data concentration. Facilities are shared at all time, and traffic is active and instantaneous. One result of great potential impact is the disconnection between sender and receiver.

Advantages of packet switching are the following:

High transmission facility utilization

Flexible network routing

Flexibility of message handling irrespective of the type of message

Minimal network transit delay

Low degree of susceptibility to many types of network failures, hence, high reliability and very low error rates

Output terminals buffered by the network from the input terminals

Flow control minimizes network or nodal congestion, journaling, statistics

Packet switching also has its disadvantages. Among them are an elaborate setup, the need for software support, and a rather costly network which must be used as near to capacity as possible.

As a final note, let us discuss briefly pacuit switching, hybrid version of packet switching and circuit switching. Pacuit creates packets of information at different points, then uses the techniques of statistical time-division multiplexing. It provides packet creation and switching at source and destination nodes, while it follows circuit switching technology at all intervening nodes.

Table 9.2
The Three Types of Switching Contrasted

Criteria	Circuit Switching	Message Switching	Packet Switching
1. General purpose	x		x
2. Physical connection	x		
3. Logical connection		x	x
4. Real time (classical)	x		
5. Secondary storage		x	x
6. Easy saturation	x		
7. Rerouting		x	x
8. Long setup	x		
9. Cumulative delays		x	x
10. Error control		x	x
11. Speed conversion		x	x
12. Code conversion		x	x
13. Multiaddress		x	x
14. Throughput		x	x
15. Good line usage		x	x
16. Diversity of devices	x		x
17. Flexibility		(x)	x
18. Growth possibilities			x

The division is good for 1979–80.

Circuit pre-establishment is required. As a result, pacuit does not offer instantaneous routing flexibility (hence, no true interactivity), but it does ensure the delay minimization features of circuit switching. The fact of using circuit switching approaches ensures that pacuit does not provide end-to-end electronic data communication or store and forward between nodes, though it does ensure error protection from DTE to node and from node to DTE.

Pacuit allows for lower speed transmission links between nodes than does packet switching. Rather than building queues, it builds time-slot links via a software table. The DTE-to-DTE communication is through virtual circuits.

Comparison of the Three Basic Methods

Having discussed the basic characteristics of packet switching, we can now outline the primary features characterizing this procedure. The features may be regrouped into twelve major points: (1) principal line control protocol for recent teleprocessing products; (2) two-way simultaneous transmission of data (full duplex); (3) transmission of code-independent (including character length) information; (4) full information transparency; (5) higher throughput rate than earlier protocols. Some of the technical features regard flexibility: (6) can be extended for satellite communications; (7) applicable to existing common carrier facilities; and (8) can be utilized primarily in polled networks, asymmetric networks which include one primary station and one or more secondary stations, and symmetric networks. Then there are the dependability and efficiency characteristics: (9) full error detection; (10) automatic retransmission ability; (11) piggyback implied acknowledgment; and (12) ability to interleave information, programs, and supervisory control messages.

We said that packet switching has been an evolutionary process largely influenced by message-switching experiences. Table 9.1 presents a comparison of technical and use-oriented factors between packet switching and its predecessors.

Finally, Table 9.2, in a brief but comprehensive manner, uses eighteen basic criteria to contrast the three methods of switching.

10

Implications for a Packet-Switching Network

There are several implications in current trends in network architecture and in the protocols which have been advanced and implemented.

First, designers should separate the communications and networking functions from applications characteristics. They should dedicate a set of processors to network functions—and not let the applications get mixed up in them.

Second, designers should integrate separate networks to reduce the redundancy of communications facilities throughout the organization. To do this, the network should support a variety of processors and terminals operating diverse applications. Designers should plan to provide a rich variety of services and service levels within the network to create a common ground with multiple potential uses. This answers the dual purpose of economy and optimization, the latter with reference to the possible communications paths needed to foster a free-flowing interchange of information.

Third, designers should maximize architectural and protocol compatibility to make such diverse elements work together. One way to manage diversity and change is to set up a generalized network with application orientation accomplished through layers of terminal hardware and control protocols.

But designers should also realize that successful utilization of a network relies largely on the method by which a device gains access to the communications medium, including communications controllers, channels, and disciplines, couplers, switching elements, and distribution elements.

Modern communications controllers are software-oriented devices dedicated to communications control, for instance front ends, remote concentrators, and network monitors.

Communications channels can be leased private wire teletypewriter, typewriter exchange service (TWX), Telex, multistation leased narrowband systems (roll-call polling), leased voice-band services, and the public switched telephone network.

121

This last comes in a number of alternatives, such as direct distance dial, foreign exchange, wide-area telecommunications (WATS), and the Bell Data-phone 50 service (50 kilobit switched service). Among the specialized common carrier services are Western Union broadband, Telenet, Tymnet, Infonet, Western Tele-communications, specialized record carriers (RCA, etc.) for international data traffic, and private microwave links.

Communications disciplines aim to provide more efficient use of the existing physical facilities. They do so by subdividing communications channels; examples are frequency-division multiplexing, FDM, and time-division multiplexing, TDM.

Communications couplers are the DCE (data sets, modems), direct couplers, and acoustic couplers.

The switching function is performed through one of the methods described in chapter 9. Local distribution is accomplished by means of cables, optical fibers, laser links, and local loop radio links. Wide-area data distribution is also performed by cable (long lines, undersea, etc.), by radio links—and, for the next decade, by satellites.

As the functions, the methods, and the media interleave and interact with one another, the network—and its architects—will be involved with a whole range of issues from the physical devices to the grand design. The clay in their hands will be man-made conventions and devices (Figure 10.1). Both would be more valuable if the users as well as the specialists could understand them.

Connectivity

Let us assume that the choice has been made to use packet switching. Computers must be selected to implement the switching and its communication functions, which include store and forward, routing, switch monitoring, line concentrating, reliability, redundancy evaluation, error and terminal handling. Other computer-performed functions are response control, information display, priority handling, security assurance, statistical loading calculations, and customer billing.

An architectural design aims at the above faculties, some of which fall into the network area, others into the systems (applications) domain, and several are borderline cases between the two classes. Which are the specific technical issues the architect must resolve in order to implement packet switching? The technical issues requiring solution include connectivity, terminal support, topology, and network organization.

Typically, the connectivity, i.e., the number of line ends per node, of first-generation networks has been between two and three. However, a higher con-nectivity is desirable to provide minimum transit delay through the network and to ensure high reliability. The early (1972) Arpanet design called for a connectivity of 2.23. Arpanet connectivity was increased gradually primarily to provide sufficient reliability; today it is approximately 2.75. However, this added connectivity results in a network utilization of only 30 percent during peak periods.

Figure 10.1
Man-made conventions and devices and their implementation

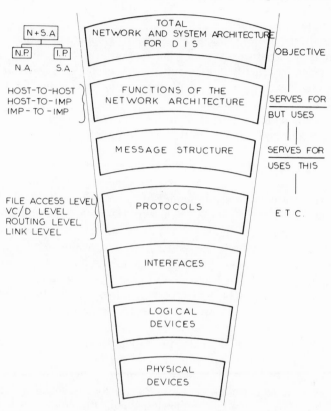

Supporting low-speed terminals and dial ports directly from an unduplexed minicomputer gives the kind of reliability noted in the Arpanet—0.72 percent unavailability. This, in general, is unacceptable to many customers; it is therefore desirable to support the terminals from a duplexed minicomputer. But to duplex all minicomputer terminal ports is economically unprofitable. Hence, these low-speed ports are first concentrated by means of a time-division multiplexer onto a high-speed line; low-speed ports may be switched en masse to a standby minicomputer if the primary minicomputer fails. This results in high port availability without unnecessary duplication of terminal ports, e.g., 0.01 percent port unavilability. It also provides the option of extending the service to small users, outside the cities served with minicomputer packet switches, at only the cost of a duplexed time-division multiplexer and one or two access lines back to the large city.

The topology of modern packet networks is a two-level hierarchy. The nodes of the top level are small, highly interconnected packet switching subnetworks of minicomputers. Due to this and standby minicomputers at each site, the switching nodes are extremely reliable, far more so than an individual duplexed minicomputer. The network topology must answer subscriber needs, which leads to the provision of microprocessor solutions able to ensure that users and potential users can hook up to the network.

We can distinguish two basic topological configurations. The first is the small asysnchronous concentrator, an inexpensive statistical concentrator permitting multiple asynchronous ports of 50 to 300 bits per second to be concentrated onto, say, a line of 1,800 bits per second. Its uses are for small cities, host computer interfacing, and terminal clusters.

The second configuration is the host interface concentrator. This can concentrate asynchronous host computer ports onto one or more synchronous access lines using, for instance, the X.25 protocol. It is used primarily for interfacing host computers to the network when the host does not support X.25 directly. The packet-switching node supports many varieties of terminal and host computer protocols, including packet assembly and disassembly functions. The node interconnects with the rest of the network using the X.25 protocol via multiple network lines.

The microprocessor hardware consists mainly of line cards, each having 4 or 8 asynchronous and/or synchronous ports, a microprocessor, local memory, and connection to two data transfer buses. Each card has sufficient processing power to handle the line protocol (X.24, XDLC, BSC, polled, asynchronous) for all its ports and to assemble or disassemble buffers of data. It then transfers the data blocks to a large buffer area in main memory; dual microprocessor central processor units then route the data to the output line card and take care of connection management and other supervisory tasks. The dedicated processing power and memory available on each line card ensures the responsiveness and reliability of the system even with heavy loads, complex protocols, and large numbers of lines.

The network organization is impacted by the availability of the multi-microcomputer switch. First, a completely redundant multi-microcomputer-based packet-switching node supporting the full range of port speeds and protocols costs less than half that of its minicomputer predecessors. It may be installed extensively in smaller cities. Where the full packet switch is not economical, the small asynchronous concentrator can be used, producing error-controlled, concentrated access at a cost which is less than that of multiplexers or minicomputer-based concentrators.

The second impact of microprocessors is the high reliability due to the redundant multi-microcomputer design and the ability to interconnect the switches into the network, creating a third level of hierarchy.

Benefits of a Packet-Switching Network

Now let us look at the benefits of packet switching. What will the user organization obtain as a result of the efforts of its designers and the costs management has supported?

Computers are recognized as the major element in any sizable information system because of their ability to process data at electronic speeds. However, the functions of distributing and dispatching the information cannot be handled by the computer as we have known it for over twenty-five years. Between the user of the information and the supplier some adequate distribution channel must be provided. This is the role of a data transmission network.

The distribution of computerized information has always used the infrastructure of other distribution processes: printout from a computer can be mailed by regular postal services, magnetic tapes containing millions of characters are regularly airmailed across the world, and new services, such as Teletext, use the television network to distribute data along with image. Other services, like Viewdata, use the telephone network to pump data into the television set of every home, and also allow two-way communications. However, the telephone network is by far the most obvious network used in data transmission. Almost any computer can transmit and receive data over a telephone line.

Faced with providing remote access to an interactive computer system, the data communications planner typically looks at the amount of usage expected from various remote locations, and compares the economies of building a leased private-line network versus using conventional public circuit-switching facilities.

Today, the public packet network is technologically superior in many respects to a private-line network because of such characteristics as the following.

It adapts to changing and often unpredictable terminal communication requirements, such as new locations, increased traffic loads, new types of terminal equipment, and new applications.

It has higher quality service than is possible in the typical private-line network.

It reduces the direct costs for communications and makes better utilization of the company's computers, terminals, and staff resources.

It eliminates many of the housekeeping chores associated with network management, such as selecting equipment with multiple vendors, maintaining the system, and monitoring network utilization and performance.

Peak traffic loads can be handled easily. Bandwidth, sequencing, delay, error rate, bit stream/packet, broadcast or point-to-point, multidestination, and capacity allocation have been studied with traffic load in mind.

In terms of topology, adding terminals in new locations requires no major effort at all on the user's part.

A great advantage is flexibility. The typical private network offers access to only one computer center. But the public packet network permits any terminal to access any computer system on the network.

It offers higher availability and quality of service, powerful error detection and correction techniques, and economic factors from original investment to operations.

The design, implementation, operation, and maintenance of a nationwide private data communications network would require a considerable amount of company resources. It is necessary to forecast uncertain traffic volume, recruit data communications specialists, consider network design alternatives (modems, multiplexers, minicomputers, programmable concentrators), evaluate different procedural solutions (roll call, hub polling, contention), and incur capital investments costs for equipment. Network management costs for such tasks are sometimes as large as the direct costs for network line facilities. A public packet-switching network already performs these functions on behalf of the user.

Packet-switching networks are designed to operate in the real world where telephone lines fail, and "standards" are not standard at all. Current packet-switching technology guarantees no more than one bad bit of information over four billion bits transmitted.

Value-Added Services

The value-added services—offered by value-added networks (VAN)—include error detection and correction, hence, dependability; adaption of a variety of terminal devices, transmission codes, protocols, and speeds; modems, circuit switches or packet switches, hosts, terminals, application software may be provided by the VAN, as well as the protocol layer, including line-control procedures, circuit setup, interfaces, terminal-to-host and host-to-host protocols; complete accounting and statistical information; security and protection; store and forward; gateway capability.

Among all the characteristics of a gateway, flexibility is probably the most important. A gateway must cope with actual and future requirements in terms of capacity, handling of various protocols, speed, and copying with various accounting parameters.

Flexibility is vital. Over leased lines of 9,600 bits per second, technology allows up to 192 simultaneous communications at speeds from 110 to 1,200 bits per second. Tymnet is an example. But flexibility will not come as a matter of course. The design objectives for the system must be settled properly, and the obvious place to begin is with the goals. The service goals should be examined, functional and applications performance characteristics identified, and a preliminary choice of transmission media made. This involves the analysis of physical transmission paths and choices among types of uses and methods of obtaining a good communications service.

The choice of the switching method is closely related to that of the transmission media. It involves both physical and logical aspects, and it has cost aftermaths as it impacts the use and sharing of the transmission paths in the data communications network.

Specifications should be developed for each of these issues, by defining performance requirements, topology functions, equipment, and interfaces.

Protocol design is closely related to these functions, and so are the interface characteristics. The ability to handle mass data transfers, such as those between computers or between high-speed terminals and computers, must come from

Table 10.1

1. In studying user statistics, you must establish:
    Peak Month
    Peak day
    Peak hour

The yearly mean is not a representative base of reference.

2. In examining total time, a distinction must be made among:
    Machine turnaround
    Line turnaround
    Data input
    Data output
    (-Man-to-man communication)

---

increased node processing speed. To virtually remove this factor as a network limitation, it is necessary to implement a design that can modularly cluster these nodes, interconnecting as many as are appropriate, to achieve a bandwidth objective with a transfer mechanism that makes the cluster behave like a multiprocess computer operating on a single memory. Then the ability to connect clusters together over as many parallel communications lines (56 KBPS) as are required over any given route gives the network virtually limitless bandwidth capability.

Earlier, we defined the backbone of the packet-switching network as composed of (1) nodes communicating with other nodes, hosts, terminals, or clusters, and (2) lines.

Node-to-node communication may be partitioned into several distinct functions: line interface, buffer management, process interface, and supervisory activities.

A supervisory record may be 48 bits long, as in Tymnet. It travels along the data route. This exchange of supervisory records is transparent to the user.

Routing overhead comes from three sources: nodes report any links that are out, i.e., that do not send a supervisory record every, say, 16 seconds; supervisory records instruct the receiving node(s) to change the permuter tables—and such instructions must be executed; the acknowledgment of these changes.

Such operations take place without any particular concern to the user whose primary interest is with the system architecture rather than the network architecture. This is the basic benefit which causes interest in the services of a value-added network.

Delay Analysis

Whether the network to be built is based on circuit-, message-, or packet-switching principles, a fundamental design requirement is delay analysis. Two prerequisites come immediately to mind: (1) the use of statistics (Table 10.1), current and

Figure 10.2
Networkwide view

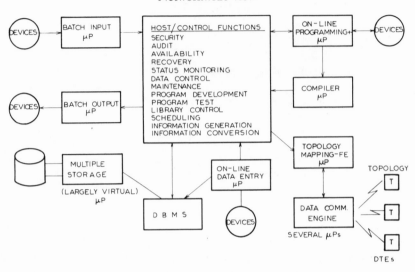

estimated or simulated, and (2) a networkwide view, including all possible functions devices, supports, and interactions (Figure 10.2). Software is also an evident requirement but the wise person would be on the lookout to convert as many functions as possible to microprocessors.

Let us start once again with the fundamentals. The delay suffered by a packet in the communication network is defined as the elapsed time between the receipt of the last bit of a packet by the source node and the delivery of its last bit to the destination node.

Delay for a circuit is the algebraic sum of the delays for each process the data must pass through. This is broken into end points and links. At the terminal interface, delay depends on the host process. For the links along the paths, it is solely dependent on the line speed except for anomalous situations involving line errors requiring retransmission.

Link delay is composed of three parts: switch time at the source, the destination, and the tandem nodes; propagation time over the internodel links; queueing time in front of the internodal links (Figure 10.3).

Switch delay has two components: waiting time for a processor to become available, and the actual processing time. Switch delay is independent of the length and type of packets (priority or normal), and it is negligible at the tandem node (order of 1 to 3 seconds).

The optimization of data transfer times requires a delay analysis. This, in turn, brings into evidence the need to study the arrival distribution with messages created outside the network and from a variety of sources. Examples are sales and mechandising through the use of point-of-sale equipment, bank tellers on-line to

Figure 10.3

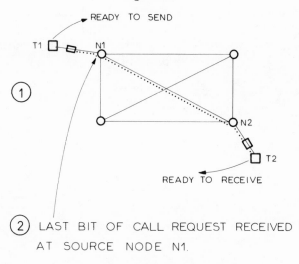

READY TO SEND

T1 N1

①

N2

T2

READY TO RECEIVE

② LAST BIT OF CALL REQUEST RECEIVED
AT SOURCE NODE N1.

③ NETWORK DELAY TIME
(TRANSIT)

network and central resources, programs on minicomputers requiring information from files stored on other machines.

Typical cases which have been examined involve generation and packetizing of messages on local equipment, submitting of messages (to the network), transfer of messages (by the network), queuing of messages (at the network), and delivery of messages to destination.

A service-time distribution (queuing model) must be created, and this is essentially determined by the distribution of packet lengths, and the capacity of the links over which they are to be transmitted. When a packet of "L" bits in length is transmitted over a link with a capacity of "C" bits per second, the time required is "L/C" seconds.

The bits associated with control, addressing, and error checking are in addition to the user data. They constitute a fixed overhead associated with each packet handled by the network.

Obtaining Better Service

The key issue in a systems study is the service provided to the end user; see Figure 10.4. Better service includes the speed of communications and the throughput.

"Turnaround" is a dynamic measure indicating the delay between the presentation of input to a system and the receipt of output from it, given the job stream

Figure 10.4
Delay analysis must consider "DTE-N-N-DTE" and study both terminal and internode traffic, including queues, propagation, and buffering. Model assumes FIFO procedure (not necessarily correct with priorities). Delay performance: 90th percentile.

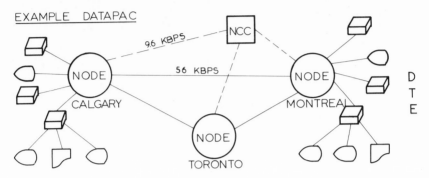

EXAMPLE DATAPAC

within which it operates. We may distinguish foreground (network) and background—or computer turnaround times. For a given communications network, low delay requirements oblige smaller message size, faster lines, and fewer node-to-node hops.

Delay studies involve elements in parallel. Queuing delay is a function of the network load. Processing delay at the switching nodes is largely related to the store-and-forward and error-detection facilities. Message delay is proportional to the size of the message and inversely proportional to the bandwidth. Delay proper is a function of the distance of the transmission circuit.

Throughput is usually measured by the peak traffic level supported; specifically it measures the steady-state work capacity of the system and the time necessary for the processing of a defined work load. The study of throughput is an examination of network elements arranged in a series. Throughput is determined by the slowest component in the system, which acts as the bottleneck. High throughput requirements suggest bigger packet size, lower packet overhead, and a greater number of alternative paths. Design must balance these features.

Electrical (or other, optical, etc.) characteristics, signal disciplines, message formats, and bandwidth available, all have an impact on delay and throughput.

Also important to obtaining better service is the measurement of the intensity of the traffic. The traffic unit recommended by CCITT is the Erlang.* As a unit of measure, it involves two basic variables: the number of circuits contemporaneously occupied in an instant "t," and use availability based on the statistical data of the actual telephone (voice, data) traffic. The number of Erlang which passes in one hour in the circuit, represents the percentage of time in which the circuit remains occupied.

*International Telephone and Telegraph Consultative Committee. These standards are usually implemented in Europe.

$N \cdot t_m = A$

For instance, 0.3 Erlang indicates that "this circuit" is occupied 30 percent of the time.

The medium intensity of traffic, expressed in Erlang, is equal to the product of the total number, "N," of communications at peak hours, multiplied by the average time t_m, of each. It is like a cascade: successive accessibility, for instance, to 10 successive levels.

The impact of delay is relative to the application. Certain types of applications require low delay for satisfactory response time, a typical case being inquiry response. Short or negligible delays can be bought at a higher cost. Thus, the study must be all inclusive, with cost effectiveness as a prime requirement.

Delay Performance with Datapac

For the Datapac network, the delay performance is specified in terms of the average delay, as well as the 90th percentile delay (90 percent of the packets are delayed less than T seconds). This is done for priority packets and for normal packets.

To estimate 90th percentile delays, a knowledge of the actual delay distributions (or suitable approximations) for priority and normal packets is necessary. Carefully kept statistics and simulation studies help. The queuing time and transmission time are taken as a function of the type of packet (priority or normal) and its length.

In general, messages are generated outside the network by a variety of sources—point of sales, banking terminals, inventory control applications. As the messages are generated, they are packetized and the resulting packets are submitted to the network at the sender node. There they are processed and placed in the appropriate queue for transmission. In case the packets arrive at a network node from a large number of independent sources over relatively low-speed access links, the arrival distributions for the priority and normal packets may be modeled by independent Poisson processes with appropriate parameters.

At each link in the network, priority packets are given preference over normal packets for transmission. To further advance the communications speed, the maximum allowable size of priority packets is 128 bytes, as compared to 256 bytes for normal packets. The priority class is primarily intended for inquiry–response or interactive applications for which near real-time delivery is a prerequisite. Transmission speed is less critical for the normal class of service, since it caters to less time-critical applications, such as bulk data transfer and remote job entry.

11

Error Detection and Correction

To perform failure recovery correctly and achieve a good data communications environment, we must deal very precisely with the control of errors. Several methods exist for error control over a communications facility. A practical and effective approach incorporates into the design an error-detection mechanism and provides for retransmission by the sender.

Retransmission can be initiated by a negative acknowledgment (NAK) from the destination when it does not receive the intended message, or a positive acknowledgment (ACK) from the destination when it does receive the message and a time-out device in the origin. This way, the origin will retransmit the message when it fails to receive a positive acknowledgment and the time has run out. The second solution is preferred with the newer protocols such as the bit-oriented XDLC.

The designer must decide how much error control the system should offer. A little? Error detection by means of check bits? A complete error control service? The last sounds preferable, but is costly.

As a general rule, if an error is detected, the message is erroneous. However, not detecting an error does not necessarily mean that the message is correct.

Communications errors within an XDLC operation may be classified into three categories.

Network detectable, but not recoverable. These result in virtual circuit resets.

Network detectable, and recoverable. There is no reason to disconnect or repeat.

Network undetectable (and unrecoverable) due to a deficiency of the error-control algorithm.

To ensure that the receiver did indeed receive the information sent by the transmitter, a cyclical redundancy check is performed. The transmitter calculates the frame check sequence (FCS) upon the address, control, and information fields as they are about to be transmitted. The resulting FCS is included in the transmitted frame. The destination, using the same polynominal controls, compares the result with the FCS sent from the origin. If these results are equal, the frame is accepted. If not, it is rejected.

The error control procedure must strike a balance between cost and security. Retransmission also means cost, delay, lower throughput, and greater possibility of error. With packet switching, error control costs on the average ± 1 percent of the budget.

Errors and the Systems View

Errors will never be really corrected—much less eliminated—until a systems view is taken of the data communications problem. A system is a set of components with their interrelationships designed to provide a specified service. The components of the system can themselves be systems. Their interrelationships comprise the algorithm of the system. To complicate matters a little, there is no requirement that a component provides service to a single system; it may be a component of several distinct systems.

The algorithm is specific to each system individually. The error-free behavior of a system is a measure of the success by which it conforms to predefined specifications. Without such specifications nothing may be said about errors, their causes, and the way to control them. Deviation of a system from its specified behavior is called a failure. Various formal measures related to an error-free performance may be based on the actual or predicted incidence of errors and their consequences.

Systems are never completely error free; they meet their specifications for a fraction of time. Errors may be permanent or transient, and the extent of the damage which they produce may be localized or distributed. Since errors are items of information, error detection and error recovery are issues that help ensure dependability. Errors are not extraneous and misdirected events, but an integral part of the process. Their importance is comparable to the other intended critical factors of a system.

A fault is not an error. It is something generic to the mechanical or algorithmic construction characterizing the system. Under some circumstances faults will cause the systems to assume an erroneous state. Furthermore, because the service provided by a system is related to one or more environments, fault-tolerant systems differ with respect to their behavior in the presence of a fault. If the aim is to continue to provide a fraction of the full performance and capabilities until the fault is removed, we speak of "fail-soft" solutions.

Error Reduction

No matter which DTE a user chooses, he wants to be sure that it can support a data control faculty. Errors may come from a simple, keying activity (e.g., errors made by the operator working on the keyboard), from the equipment itself (machine errors), from the transmission line (usually, noise*), or from other equipment communicating with this DTE.

A DTE must provide, through hardware or software, the needed controls to check and correct errors. Error detection had been performed by a variety of means, the two most popular being parity check and hash total.

Parity check is where an extra bit or byte, called a check digit, is added at the end of the message-carrying digits, and controlled against a pre-established algorithm. If to the number 12345 is added a check digit—say, odd/even type: $1 + 3 + 5 = 8$; $-2 + 4 = 6$, and $8 - 6 = 2$—then the number will be written 123452. The last digit, "2," is for control purposes. If the operator inputs by mistake 132452, the machine will do the above calculation, establish that 13245 does not correspond to the check digit "2," and signal an error.

Hash Total is simply a summation of the fields used for checking purposes which has no other meaning than to permit the receiver to check the numbers in a lot against it and accept or reject the lot as a whole. The hash total, or squaring control, is applicable to data entered in the numerical fields. Its object is to check if a list (block of data) has been input correctly by the operator, if an error in keying has been made, or if a figure has been lost in transmission. (The ability of a terminal to respond is generally known as visual input check. The possibility for checking the input data, as it is keyed, must be complemented by that of a feedback to the operator. This is usually carried out through the printing of the text itself or through its visualization.)

But these classic approaches, parity check and hash total, are obsolete for today's large-scale communications requirements. They imply high cost, significant redundancy, and low dependability because of compensating errors, while the noise in the transmission does not always last the length of one single bit. For these reasons, error control through polynomial error checks is much more efficient.

Unbuffered terminals, however, still need old parity checks. In fact, the best error control an unbuffered terminal can achieve is the detection of an error through some parity check. Buffered terminals can detect errors and call for retransmissions, but only if they know how to notify each other about errors and recognize the requests for retransmission. A protocol is required. Fault isolation becomes easier, too, since the protocol provides a means of identifying the source of errors.

Error control must involve control of field† length, detection of the omission of fields, and assurance of the total introduction of a field. These are applicable to data input, data transmission and the reception of messages. The utilization of terminals, which allows control of data in transmission, is of great importance in a data communications environment.

Key issues relate to format, that is, the way the data is organized and presented on hard copy or through visualization. Format controls may be obtained by means of software. Other cases are the following:

*Noise is any unwanted input.
†A set of one or more characters, not necessarily lying in the same word, which is treated as a whole; a unit of information.

Preventing an alphabetical field from invading a numerical zone (the assurance that in a numerical zone there are no alphabetical characters)

Determining whether a numerical zone should be subject to parity checks or hash totals

Verifying a functional sequence

Normalizing a zone (the word "normalizing" should be interpreted with reference to the operations which follow and their requirements, for instance, data transmission, handling by another computer)

Carrying out functions such as perforating, printing, read–write on cassette, and the like

Insertion or deletion of specific fields of data into the records stored in memory.

Control possibilities may exist at different levels of sophistication. Their presences make the terminals very different from one another, therefore constituting a parameter* which must be considered most carefully in a comparative analysis.

We must also consider the management of the output data, generally known as editing. † Editing is done mostly through software: for intelligent terminals it is done by their own programs and for other terminals it is done through commands transmitted on-line from a computer, minicomputer, or microcomputer. In either case, the aim is to formalize and direct the handling of data by editing the fields; injecting (or, alternatively, suppressing) blanks, zeros, punctuation signs; using service characters to structure the printed (or visualized) output; returning the carriage to the origin; controlling the paper feed (for instance, skipping or jumping lines); printing on different modules depending on the nature of the data; and varying the position of the printer on the printing lines.

A terminal that allows the aforementioned kinds of data management will be that much more useful to the person or organization faced with specific editing problems. On the other hand, such terminals are expensive.

An Integrated Approach to EDC

Error detection and correction, EDC, protocols are very important with transaction-oriented interactive environments and heavy data loads. Error messages must be generated for all machines, programs, operator errors, and operational information.

Error status and statistical data must be recorded in a dedicated storage device (for instance, a diskette), printed upon operator command via an "error retrieve" routine, or made available on video. Error recording and subsequent printed error history should be provided for the central processing unit, timers, input–output channels, and devices, storage devices, and operator stations.

---

*A quantity to which arbitrary values may be assigned; used in subroutines and generators to specify item size, decimal point, block arrangement, field length, sign position, etc.

†The arrangement of information; it may involve the deletion of unwanted data, the selection of pertinent data, the insertion of information prior to printing, zero suppression, etc.

Programmed diagnostic tools must be available to help in problem isolation. Users should be given extensive training, documentation, and hands-on experience in the application of diagnostics.

Error reduction presupposes concrete policies (and policing) to ensure that they are put into action. Error detection and retransmission techniques require automatic request for repetition, ARQ. This has become a standard error-recovery technique utilized for both half-duplex and full-duplex protocols.

To sum up, error recovery techniques should cover all information, not just the data part of a message. Messages may contain information pertaining to file organization, data type, format, record attributes, record length, size, device characteristics, or other data relevant to protection and characterization of the file systems involved. If a piece of data is important enough to communicate it, it is also important to protect it from errors.

The Cyclic Redundancy Check

The cyclic redundancy check (CRC) polynominal is a 16-bit check providing an undetected error rate less than $1 \times 10 - 12$ per bit. This is the basic error protection algorithm in packet switching.

The frame check sequence (FCS) field is a 16-bit cyclic redundancy check of all data in the XDLC frame except the opening and closing flag fields and any zero insertion. The transmitter performs the computation and sends the FCS field. The receiver performs the identical computation, discarding the frame if it is in error and does not advance its count. More precisely, the transmitter indicates its 16-bit trailer. The binary value of the trailer is calculated on the basis of a multiplication by x^{16}, then division by the generating polynomial, $x^{16} + x^{12} + x^5 + 1$. The integer content digits are ignored. The transmitter sends the complement of the resulting remainder value; high-order bits are transmitted first. The expected error performance is the detection of all odd numbers of errors in the frame and any error burst less than 16 bits in length. This is done in hardware because time for software handling is 16 milliseconds.

Other error-detection mechanisms are longitudinal redundancy check (LRC), a parity check applied to certain bit positions in every character in a block; vertical redundancy check (VRC), a parity check applied to all bit positions in one character; and data complement, a data verification technique employing one complement (inverted) check bit for every information bit.

Bit Error Rate

The most important performance criterion of a data transmission link is the measure of the quantity of errors the system introduces on the average, that is to say, how large the bit error rate, BER, or the probability of error, $P(e)$, is.

BER is the number of erroneous bits verified in a bit string. This defines the quality of transmission. Experimentally, the BER is measured and defined by the equation

$$\text{BER} = \frac{N}{N_t} = \frac{N_c}{B_{t_o}}$$

Where N_e = number of bit errors in a time interval t_o

N_t = total number of transmitted bits in t_o

B = bit error rate of the binary source

t_o = measuring time interval, i.e., error counting time

BER is used to indicate the number of errors in the handling of bits given by a piece of equipment or transmission line. As a unit of measurement, it reflects the dependability of a communications link. For instance, in a given network 300 baud lines commit 1 bit error on 10,000 bits transmitted—hence, 10^{-4} BER; 1,200 baud lines commit 1 bit error on 1,000 bits transmitted—hence, 10^{-3} BER. For a random, stationary error-generation process and sufficiently long measurement interval t_o, the measured BER gives an estimate of the true $P(e)$.

As an example of the influence of environmental factors, for a given piece of equipment there is BER degradation due to temperature variations.* Temperature acts as an agent and affects degradation of circuits and the life cycle of the terminals.

The evaluation of probability of error, $P(e)$, of nonoperational (out of service) channels is a well-known measurement technique. Performance evaluation of such systems is done with a pseudo-random test signal sequence transmitted through the measured channel. The receiver computes the $P(e)$ by comparing the received bits with a stored replica of the transmitted bit pattern. The main problem associated with simple nonoperational BER measurements is that it is not feasible to evaluate the performance of an operating system carrying the unknown digital data stream of the customer.

Operation of an automatic phase-tracking system requires three main elements: a fast error monitor to detect the better channel (the pseudo-error monitor); an error-free data switch to select the better channel; and a means of maintaining the two paths in phase with each other to eliminate switching errors.

Let us see the features built for a data above voice, DAV, system used for multiplexing of voice and data. The pseudo-error detector provides an accurate estimate of the data system error rate at all times, and by operating on 1.5 megabits per second without adding or using any more bits is highly efficient and very rapid. Since it uses an error-multiplication technique, a predicted error rate of, say, 10^{-8} can be read out of the pseudo-error detector before errors have actually occurred in the main data path.

Apart from the normal built-in fault monitors, a means is necessary to determine if real data continuity is maintained throughout the system. This is

---

*The amount of level drift is about 1.5 decibels over the 0°C–50°C range, and is almost totally dependent on the performance degradation of the modulator/demodulator (data set).

achieved by monitoring the multiplex framing bits in the 1.5 megabits per second data stream. By employing techniques to avoid ambiguities in the reporting of loss of framing bits, a subtle failure may be rapidly pinpointed to a particular piece of equipment and the transmission of random, but totally false, data can be avoided.

Four methods exist for generating pseudo-error characteristics: shifted detection threshold, intersymbol interference enhancement, noise addition, and sampling phase offset. Practical conditions generally govern the choice of method.

Error Rate and the Dependability of Carriers

In-service and on-line monitoring may be achieved with test sequence interleaving, parity check coding, code violation detection, and pseudo-error detection.

Pseudo-error detection techniques remove both the shortcomings of long evaluation time and the requirements to interrupt data traffic of nonoperating systems. For pseudo-error detection a "secondary" decision device is connected in parallel with the main data path. This secondary path has intentionally degraded performance and its output sequence has an error rate much greater than the unknown error rate of the main receiver. This amplified error rate is obtained by taking the main receiver output data as a reference and counting the number of disagreements with respect to the secondary output data stream. Every disagreement is called pseudo-error.

The two most important elements in the performance of a pseudo-error detector are the ability to achieve a sufficient error multiplication factor and the capacity to reach a stable multiplication factor in the presence of nongaussian perturbations. A pseudo-error device must be tested to determine its ability to detect burst perturbation in the input signal to the phase shift key (PSK) modulator and demodulator. Such bursts (clusters of errors) may arise in certain nonideal transmission systems and include signal interruptions noise bursts, tone bursts, and a combination of these.

Since some of the possible solutions to one problem result in a degradation of capabilities available to solve the other problems, efficiency compensation, and error control must be studied to yield a useful compromise between performance and cost of the communication terminal (modem).

Current technology permits the following solutions: Noise found in telephone and, generally, communication channels tends to bring about clusters of errors. These bursts may be handled by an interleaving technique, which has the effect of splitting the bursts into isolated errors with many correct bits in between. The isolated errors are then easily handled, for example, by a simple current code.

Recurrent codes, also called convolutional codes, do not have a readily definable block structure. Check bits are periodically inserted and always depend on the same pattern as preceding information bits. With this scheme, mean time between errors is improved by two or three orders of magnitude with only modestly complex equipment.

We must stress the fact that current knowledge of the dependability of common carrier systems and facilities and of the techniques for modeling this reliability is far from satisfactory. Possible causes of system failure reside in switching systems, long- and short-haul carriers, along with probable causes of short-term and long-term outages.

The impact of common carrier reliability on computer communications systems depends on the type of system being contemplated. This impact is most critical on systems that rely heavily on stringent response times where occasional failures to obtain a response in a brief time period cannot be tolerated.

In data communications practice, private-line characteristics are relatively stable, impluse noise can be reduced, and line conditioning provides more nearly ideal frequency response. However, inexplicable anomalies can occur, for example, a private line exhibiting a variation in bit error rate of 2×10^{-5} to 3×10^{-7}. Probability distribution functions for line availability and duration of failures result in rule-of-thumb summaries. They indicate a wide variation in line availability from 99.9 to 10 percent. Many line failures are repaired in a few minutes, but some persist for hours. A guide for a line selected at random to transmit data at 2,400 bits per second indicates that bit errors will occur about every 40 seconds, failures lasting 1 minute will occur every day, and a 1-hour failure will occur each month.

Control of Errors on Voice-Grade Lines

In designing data systems for use on voiceband channels, the communication engineer faces the challenge of approaching maximum channel capacity as closely as possible, within reasonable economic bounds. The problem may be organized into three distinct tasks: devise an efficient signal design to match the channel characteristics, provide automatic "equalization" or compensation for signal distortion caused by the channel, and design error-control—a means for automatically correcting data errors caused by unavoidable bursts of noise.

There are two classes of errors, each handled with a different approach. The first group is relative to the communications discipline as a whole and the one to which protocols are particularly suited. Although error control has been the subject of many protocol solutions in the last decade, it is still handled by the computer and communications industry almost uniformly in a most simple, pragmatic way. The data stream is subdivided into blocks which are augmented with enough redundant bits to afford reliable error detection. Whether it finds an error or not, the receiving terminal automatically stops after every block and briefly becomes the transmitter, sending back a message either to acknowledge receipt (ACK) or to ask for a repeat for the block (NAK). Regardless of whether the line is four-wire or two-wire, transmission is always in one direction at a time.

There is, however, an alternative to this approach. High-speed transmission proceeds in one direction while the low-speed reverse channel conveys information about the accuracy of the received data, telling the transmitting terminal to stop and repeat one or more blocks of data when an error was detected. Such uses of reverse channels have turned out to be far fewer than envisioned, and half-duplex operation still is the more common mode.

With wideband possibilities now available, the simplicity of the half-duplex operation comes at the cost of efficiency—the continual interruption of data transmission. Efficiency will especially decline in cases of long propagation delays, for example, with earth satellite channels. In such cases, it is preferable to transmit data continuously, interrupting and retransmitting only when an error has actually been detected.

The second class of errors includes those which particularly concern the transmission facility and the technology behind it. In the case of analogue signals, one of the earliest methods for combating noise was the substitution of wide-swing frequency modulation (FM) for simple amplitude modulation (AM), but, generally speaking, there are two methods of correcting errors regarding the link facility itself: the reverse-acting method and the forward-acting method.

In the reverse-acting method, the receiver only detects the presence of errors and notifies the transmitter that certain data must be repeated. This method has two disadvantages: a reverse-direction channel is required, and the data flow must be interrupted while data are transmitted.

The reverse approach is commonly used with data processing systems in which virtually all errors must be corrected. Various coding structures have been found useful. In block code, check bits are usually inserted at the end of a block of data and are determined entirely by the data bits within that block; both encoding and decoding proceeds on a block-by-block basis. In recurrent code, check bits are inserted periodically, being determined by a certain grouping of preceding information bits stretched over the so-called constraint length. There are four check bits per constraint length, producing a four-field overlap among the information-bit groupings which determine the check bits.

Interleaving techniques applicable to either type of code, use crossword puzzle arrays to rearrange data for the purpose of coding and decoding. The data flows columnwise but is encoded and decoded rowwise. Although a cluster of errors may occupy an entire column, it would affect only one bit per row. Thus, use of a single error-correcting code is sufficient.

The forward-acting method inserts enough redundant bits in the data stream before it is transmitted to allow the receiver to detect and correct most transmission errors without any interruptions. Forward-acting error correction with sophisticated codes would be practiced only if reverse communication were not feasible, but cannot give as much protection as detection-retransmission, especially during extreme channel disturbances.

With either correcting method it is essential to have a continuous knowledge of the data system error rate. Without this knowledge, the condition of the system is unknown and performance degradations in a long-haul system become very difficult to locate. Techniques have been used where known bits are added to the data stream or where some of the bits in the data stream are fixed and monitored.

Testing the Network

It is appropriate to end this chapter with a few words on testing the network. Network tests are an integral part of error-free performance and must be designed in to the system at the start of the project. The failure modes must be pre-established, and failures studied as to their aftermaths.

To support reasonably error-free environments, the network housekeeping functions must include accumulation of error statistics, automatic trouble shooting, accumulation of test statistics and test results, bit error rate testing (including bit pattern generators), link testing, accumulation of recovery statistics, automatic alternative routing, and switching alternatives.

It should be possible for each node in the network to accumulate error statistics and participate in alternative routing. Furthermore, as terminals become increasingly intelligent and equipped with microcomputers, it should also be possible to participate in network diagnostics.

12

Journaling

Many particularly important questions in distributed information systems relate to the broad and vital area of data assurance. Elaborate procedures for guaranteeing data integrity can consume a large part of a system's time and resources.

Some questions about data assurance are the following:

What is the maximum load of transactions the system can support in the presence of a given rate of failure?

How will the response time vary as a function of the failure rate?

What proportion of system time will be taken up by recovering from failures or preparing checkpoints as opposed to useful transaction processing?

How should the journal be kept to ensure recovery security and protection and still be a cost-efficient proposition?

Control responsibility, logging procedures, tests, and performance control and balancing are among the activities necessary for a sound policy of recovery procedures.

The failure of a system occurs when that system does not meet its specifications. Recovery is the restoration of the data base after a failure to a state that is acceptable to the user. A failure may be due to a deficiency in the hardware or the software, which leads to erroneous systems operation and to the pollution of the data. Failure may occur in transmission lines, or may be the intentional or unintentional introduction of erroneous information which destroys the integrity of the information stored in the computers and communications network.

To minimize lost time, a system should operate in checkpoint, rollback-recovery, CRR, mode. A consistent and complete journal should also be kept for recovery and statistical purposes; Table 12.1 presents a basic form. The logging must include the last transaction in order to know "where" to restart, and the operations

Table 12.1 Sample Journal for Distributed Recovery and Restart

Control	Logging	Audit Trail per Transaction	Shadow Updates	Image Copying	Roll-backs	Check Points	OP Backout (local)	Systems Backout
Authentication								
Sequence								
Encryption								
Timing								
Quantity								

involved at time out which might have been incomplete, interrupted, or have affected other operations. These two elements regard the quality of the recovery process. There is also the element of speed of recovery, which influences the mean time of system interrupt, MTOSI.

The Journal Is the Means

Journaling retains in one or more storage media (tape, disc) copies of information that passed through the network, and/or was delivered to intended destinations. Networks must include journaling in one or more locations because of the ability to retransmit copies of information previously delivered and the need for restart and recovery. But the maintenance of journals presents logical and physical problems as well as security.

Distributed data assurance issues involve access rights, retrieval, additions, deletions, modifications, batch perspectives, on-line responsibilities, recovery mechanism, and protocol dependencies, plus a number of data base considerations, including questions relating to the data dictionary.

Each one of these issues may be divided into a number of concrete points; for instance, retrieval involves process access, process limits, authorization, isolation by distribution and destination point, query validation, and completion testing, as well as other issues relating to the retrieval mechanism per se, such as protocol sensitivity. Additions, deletions, and modifications call for such activities as logging, audit trail, effective performance in operations, and synchronization.

It is not enough simply to maintain a journal. Information elements (IE) in the journal, such as input statistics, sequence number within the input statistics, output station, send time, receipt time, etc., must be defined a priori. Care should be taken in the collection of every item intended to help identification and retrieval.

Figures 12.1 through 12.4 detail one approach to the establishment of good journaling procedures within a data communications environment. The journaling is divided into three functions: network, data base, and overall control. Each is broken down into component parts. Among themselves they outline the functions journaling should accomplish. (Operational statistics, a part of the control function, is further exemplified by exploding it into its component parts.)

We should guarantee efficient, automatic on-line application recovery from system crashes, power failures, resource interlock between transaction, and system transaction aborts. Application recovery means transactions are not lost or entered a second time for no reason. Other requirements are imposed by the on-line environment. Journaling must provide the data needed for recovery from media failure without reentry of transactions and without errors. But a whole precedural mechanism must be set up besides the journal.

Staging delays record updates until transactions are complete so they can always be aborted with records left intact.

Figure 12.1

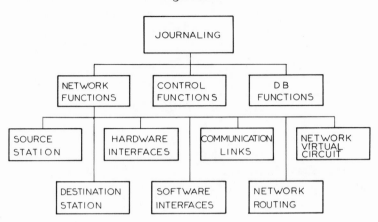

Record looking prevents simultaneous updates of records.

Security guards against unauthorized activity with user sign-ons, passwords, and identity codes.

We may also have user and terminal work classes that define what transactions are available to the user or the terminal. With distributed information systems, such grouping will usually be done at the minicomputer or work station level. But networks accept terminals of all kinds and must therefore provide the needed communications software at the user level and work class, without the prerequisite of a local intelligence.

Procedural Prerequisites

Network elements consider all information to be volatile. After a failure the software is reloaded with initial conditions, and hardware errors are cleared. Preparation of a processor for such operation involves three primary tasks: initialization—loading with no record of prior activity, checkpoint—recording dynamic status, and recovery—reinitialization using the last recorded status to resume operations. The loading of the basic software resident in the high-speed (central) memory is a responsibility of the operating system. Application-dependent functions are loaded by special software.

The requirements posed by these operations must be reflected in procedural steps to be followed in keeping the journal. Journaling is no random event, no dumping of transaction data irregardless of their importance. It is a concrete, deliberate policy followed to enhance recovery, security, and operating statistics. The journal entry must contain the (1) overhead data, which includes identification of source device (code), input sequence code, input time, message type code, output

Figure 12.2

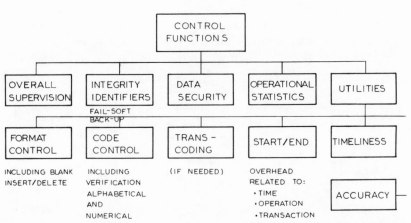

station code (destination), output sequence code, and output time, (some items, like time, may be inserted by the host processor), and (2) the message proper.

Whether centralized or decentralized, journaling has three basic purposes: storage of copies of information for reference and control, storage of intermediate data—when necessary—and retransmission, and the means of effecting re-start–recovery following a failure. The journal may also be used for statistics and billing purposes.

With centralized processing, keep the journal on disc for the first and second day. Dump on tape the n-2 journals every two days, and store the tapes in a safe place for subsequent retrieval as needed.

Distributed recovery and restart are more demanding in terms of journaling requirements. They imply the use of a systems mechanism able to perform in an efficient and uninterrupted manner logging, audit trail, shadow updates, image copying, backups, checkpoints, and backouts. They also require precise management of activities such as synchronization of maintainability, protocol choices, procedural characteristics, data base organization, studied transaction sequence, user knowledge of system behavior, and timing and precision.

The existence of a network helps substantially in automating these activities since it is impractical to mount and dismount tapes, discs, cassettes, and floppy discs all the time. One of the first and most valuable applications Citibank put on the Citinet was the automatic handling of the logging and back-up copies.

Distributed Recovery and Restart

There are five levels of recovery and restart to be studied within the overall perspective of a distributed environment:

Figure 12.3

Much valuable data can be compiled from the data base journal, e.g., frequency by type of request, receiver, files addressed, stop action, author/sender/stations, amounts handled, time in/out, recovery, etc.

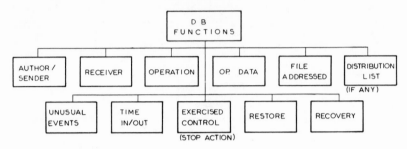

1. System recovery
2. Node recovery
3. Local process
4. Per transaction
5. Per data element (information element)

Recovery is a complex operation involving at least five procedural steps: system restart, reconfiguration (when needed), stabilization (restore), reload, and rerun. Recovery is also an expensive undertaking. Measured against the total system down time (TSDT), recovery represents, on the average, 36 percent of the TSDT.

Recovery is involved closely with the data base. The data base consists of a number of files. A file is a logical unit in the data base used to group data; an information element is the smallest logical component of a file. Recovery must reach all the way to this IE level. A recovery technique maintains data—at the IE or higher levels—to make restoration possible. It provides recovery assurance from any failure which does not affect the recovery data, the mechanisms used to maintain these data, and the techniques to restore the data in the data base.

Failures fall into two broad categories, depending on how they react to the recovery technique under examination: (1) failures with which a recovery technique can cope; these lead to a "crash" to be restored by that specific technique; (2) failures with which a recovery technique cannot cope. Such failures are called a "catastrophe," with respect to the recovery approach in question.

Every recovery mechanism is based on an understructure. This must ensure that the processes are not interfering with each other, that it is possible at any time to return a process to some previous and more acceptable state, and that it is feasible to prevent the use of created or updated information until it is known that the process will not have to be backed out. With DIS requirements are extended to controlling the process in the same or different nodes, preserving order while maintaining the structure of a distributed data base (DDB), saving results for subsequent audit to

Figure 12.4

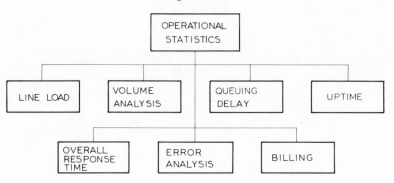

reduce the probability and significance of errors, providing repeatability of process results as required by most auditable applications.

Different types of recovery are possible for a data base:

Recovery to the correct state

Recovery to a checkpoint

Recovery to a predefined valid state (per se)

Recovery to a consistent state (within the environment)

Crash resistance

Crash resistance is provided if the normal algorithms of the system operate on the data in a manner that causes the system to always be in a correct state after certain failures. This obviates the need for the recovery techniques to cope with that class of failures by manipulating and maintaining crucial data during normal processes. Crash resistance restores states implicitly: (a) the recovery operation is "in-process" if the action was taken prior to a point of commitment, or is "post-process" if the action has been committed already. Both the in-process and the post-process recovery approaches are applications related. But if the results of processing are not yet committed, and allowance has been made only for machine errors correctable by a rerun from a checkpoint, then the operation is a systems recovery and not applications related.

The DIS environment also implies another dimension—that of ensuring restart and recovery with segmented files. But before we take on the task of segmenting files and decide what data to put on which DTE, we must study how the system will handle recovery and restart. Without a clear definition of recovery and restart, it is impossible to tackle segmentation.

Recoverability expresses the speed with which system facilities can be restored after correction of a component failure. Restoring should include the necessary correction of any data damaged as a result of the failure. The full recovery process demands effort, analysis, resources, and full knowledge of the application, since the

Figure 12.5

A transaction enters the front end with the intention to modify records A, B, and C. If Record C is write protected, records A and B have been modified prior to stopping at C. For the operation to be reversible, we must store the "before and after" image. This is a security mechanism.

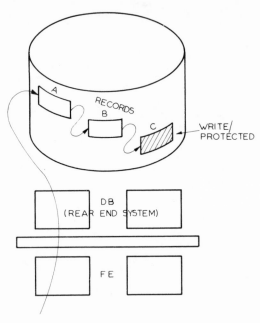

most serious effects of equipment failure are those associated with data damage. Recoverability must be designed into the system—it cannot be added on adequately after the failure. We must acknowledge from the beginning that any system component can and will fail.

Failure Isolation

For each system component—whether hardware or software—the designer must consider two basic concepts: failure isolation and provisions of aids for recovery. After assurance that the system is again operational, we must test the status of applications programs, incoming and outgoing messages, and affected data base elements, and attempt to restore them to normal operation. On recovery, checks must be made to guarantee the resumption of normal operations. Furthermore, failures are more likely to occur when the system is busy—hence, more important to the user's needs—than when it is idle.

Let us assume a front-end/rear-end organization with a transaction-oriented

Figure 12.6
Another possibility is rerouting of the transaction because of component failure. Log tape helps implement a checkpoint philosophy.

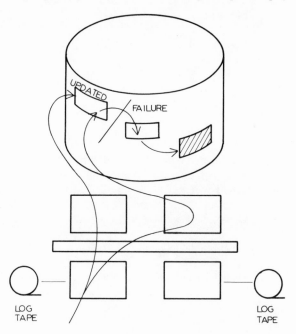

system. All activities must be journaled for recovery and auditing. A feasible strategy might be composed of the following steps:

Bring up the system, loading programs and data.

Begin execution of a program.

As work is performed, the various units of the system should monitor their own operations. Specifically, this means looking for detectable errors.

If an error occurs, a procedure must be invoked, involving retry, refreshment, and recovery.

If the error is "soft," the system is capable of recovering without any specific service activity being performed. The appropriate recovery must be accomplished and processing resumed.

If the error is "hard," no recovery is possible other than initiating a service action, which consists of identifying and diagnosing the failure, repairing the defect, verifying the repair, and returning the system to use.

Availability is increased if we identify in advance all possible failures, classify them into homogeneous groups, look out for them constantly, and work on the basis of exception reporting. Good availability strategies aim at minimizing the amount of

Table 12.2 Security Issues with DIS

Reference	Issue
Processing Unit	Frequency of recordings/check-ups
Storage Devices	Access; authorization
Distributed Entry	Dial-in, CPU, network
Network	Nodes, linkages, data bases
Protocol	Choice, control, compatibility, change
Users	How many? Where? For what purpose?
System Level	Who has access? Of what sort? How is it implemented? Where?
Journaling	Coverage, data procedural, design
Recovery	Policies to be followed, delays, dependability
Security	Higher-up authority, authentication, keys, dynamic change

A protocol for data security helps ensure that access to certain ports on the network are denied unauthorized users.

time and expense incurred to identify and diagnose the failure, repair the defect, and verify the correction and return the system to use.

A statistical function must also be performed which calls for the collection of a variety of statistics concerning the operation of the network. Such statistics may be compiled in reports hourly, daily, or in other time periods for establishing performance and information flow of the network. The statistics must include operating errors, unauthorized access attempts by priority, and authorized access or security.

Paralleling this, a utility function is needed. It involves the collection of activities not directly related to main routing, integrity, and journaling, but acts in a supporting role, for instance code translations, basic format checking such as mandatory fields, sequence numbers, etc., and destination code validation.

Security, Privacy, and Auditability

Security and privacy considerations must retain priority in the design of a distributed information system. They involve application system access, transaction access, user

Figure 12.7
Auditing functions

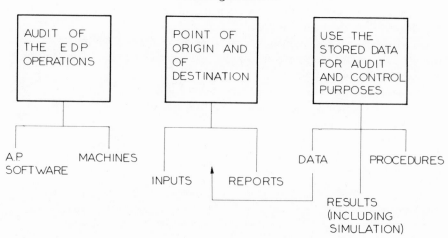

perspectives, and a distributed origin of events. The handling of such requirements presupposes both local and physical mechanisms, involving an a priori definition of access extent, system checkpoints, and application responsibilities.

Three levels of access authorization must be given in a data base system: read only (write protected), read/write, and delete. Let us look at the examples in Figures 12.5 and 12.6. A transaction entering the front end has the objective to modify records A, B, C. But record C is write protected. If operations A and B have already been performed, to reserve them we must have the "before and after" image. This procedure complements the requirements posed by the rerouting of transactions because of failure.

Both for failure and for security purposes, the distributed levels of data assurance include system, application, process unit, and data object. External and internal guarantees must be provided. These include transaction or process mapping (physical, logical), value control (fixed value, variable driven), user accessibility (transaction, passwords), and data orientation (data dictionary, data base organization, and passwords).

Passwords are defined by the data base designer (or administrator) when specifying the read, write, and delete access to the data base. But it is possible to gain access to some data without a password if the data base is designed to allow this. The distribution points (topology of hosts and terminals) must be examined, and a checklist prepared as outlined in Table 12.2.

The audit techniques which can be used for distributed auditability are static, variable, and dynamic. The way auditability is applied differs, but the functions to be performed are the same; see Figure 12.7. They include audit of EDP operations and, eventually, of the network functions, audit at point of data origin and of destination, and use of stored data for audit and control purposes.

Static approaches involve predefined controls, established processes, sampling inspections, and spot checks. Static audits must account for erroneous transactions. Generally, they do not alter the processes being audited; they are not done on-line, and they produce predefined outputs.

Variable distributed auditability also calls for predefined controls and established processes. Although it is not on-line, it does alter processes and the inputs and outputs are defined.

Finally, dynamic auditability is done on-line, deals with changeable processes, has hardly changeable inputs and outputs, involves alterable techniques, and alters the processes being audited.

All three types of auditing must create an audit trail, ensure that there is no error propagation, and last a specified time frame, being repeated in line with an established pattern within the time frame in question.

13

Life Cycle Maintainability

One of the prime concerns of the network designer is enhancement of system maintainability. What are the goals of maintainability within an on-line environment?

They are:

1. Hardware (its topology and serviceability)
2. Basic software (new releases, support of past releases)
3. Data communications (equipment installed), lines, modems, environment
4. Maintenance for applications programs packages
5. Data base management, file management, operating system for data bases
6. On-line (remote) maintenance capability

For each of these, and for the total system, contractual uptime guarantees must be provided. Systems reliability must be maintained throughout the life of the on-line system.

The total system performance entails operational, hardware, software, and communications functions. Two basic standards may be used to evaluate uptime in an objective, factual, and documented manner.

The first is system scheduled hours (uptime and downtime). The second is the system downtime resulting from different reasons. A simple algorithm reflecting this is:

$$\frac{\text{System usage time}}{\Sigma \text{ of interruptions}}$$

Unscheduled interruptions may be due to hardware failures or to other reasons as listed in Table 13.1. We measure hardware failures according to the mean time

155

Table 13.1
Performance Parameters

CALENDAR TIME					Operational	Hardware	Software	Communications
	System Uptime Hours				+	+	+	+
System Scheduled Hours	System Downtime	Hardware	Maintenance		+	+	−	−
			Dump		+	+	−	−
			Recovery		+	+	−	−
			Logistic		+	+	−	−
		Software	Patches		+	+	+	−
			Dump		+	+	+	−
			Recovery		+	+	+	−
		Unknown	Test		+	+	−	−
			Dump		+	+	−	−
			Recovery		+	+	−	−
		Operator	Dump		+	−	−	−
			Recovery		+	−	−	−
		Power Outage	Lost time		+	−	−	−
		Environment	Lost time		+	−	−	−
		Basic software	Lost time		+	+	+	−
		Maintenance error	Dump		+	+	−	−
			Recovery		+	+	−	−

CALENDAR TIME					Operational	Hardware	Software	Communications
System Scheduled Hours	System Uptime Hours				+	+	+	+
	System Downtime	Line error	Lost hours		+	+	+	+
		Modem error	Lost hours		+	+	−	−
		Supports	Lost hours		+	+	−	−
Neutral Hours	Preventive maintenance				+	+	−	−
	Power-off hours				+	−	−	−
	Idle hours				−	−	−	−

between failures, MTBF, and the mean time to repair, MTTR. But the existence of other reasons and the recovery procedures (as we shall see in the following sections) make this measure inadequate. Therefore, over the last few years, we have come to measure in terms of mean time between system interruptions, MTBSI, and mean time of system interrupt, MTOSI. All are measured in hours.

Requirements for Life Cycle Performance

MTBSI and MTOSI are much better means of evaluating the service obtained from computers and data communications systems because they reflect the combined negative effect of interruptions due to a variety of causes.

In general, it is well to remember that all types of interruptions create a prejudice. Short interruptions are software oriented, and long ones are hardware oriented. While it is easy to shut down a system, the problem is to start it up again. For performance and for stabilization computer systems should work round the clock. (But this poses a variety of other problems.)

The stress put on the computer system with every start-up has an impact on life-long performance and maintainability. With life-long maintainability are associated life cycle costs, which are the sum of acquisition, installation, operating, maintenance, logistics, and support costs. The mean time between failures and the mean time of system interrupt have a dramatic effect on life cycle costs.

The selling price of equipment at standard reliability levels is a relatively small portion of total system costs. This total system cost, related to the service to be derived from the system, decreases as the reliability increases. However, it increases very quickly as the reliability level drops. Thus, substantial savings accrue from procuring highly reliable equipment and even greater benefit from designing reliable, easy-to-maintain systems. In a certain military application, for example, switching to highly reliable equipment increased the initial cost by a factor of 2.5. But, over a ten-year period of operations, the total cost dropped from $90 million, for comparable, less reliable systems, to $30 million.

This example emphasizes the need for a long, hard look. With on-line computers and data communications systems, reliability must be studied at four levels: hosts, terminals and concentrators, city lines, and long-distance trunks.
Communications facilities are the single, most important environmental problem in today's systems and will be even more critical in the future. If terminals and line interfaces are designed properly, it should be possible to pinpoint the exact error source and switch to alternative facilities automatically, etc.

A leading European carrier noted the following four percentages of failures reported to its services:

City Lines	3%
Terminals and modems	20%
Long-distance lines	57%
Due to customer (approximate)	20%
	100%

(Host failures were of no interest to the carrier and are, therefore, not included in these statistics.)

Because system reliability is the product of the reliability of its components, $R = R_1 \times R_2 \times , \ldots , \times R_n$. This means that the weakest component (long lines) limits the overall reliability of the system. This is exactly the sore point with starlike networks and the reason for which horizontal networks with backup facilities can offer much better service.

Table 13.2 reflects a German company's experience with two terminals working on-line in a branch office. As shown, the failures occur at the same time for both terminals. Hence, it cannot be stated that the terminal itself fails—it is either the line or the central processing unit (software, hardware, or hardware/software). Whatever the cause may be—and no chain is ever more reliable than its weakest component—only a careful logging of all failures as to origin and reason can guide the designer, the user, and the organization responsible for system maintenance in improving the reliability of the on-line system.

Table 13.2 A German
Company's Experience with
Two On-line Terminals in a
Branch Office

Date of Failure	Terminal I	Terminal II
10/12	2	2
10/13	-	-
10/16	-	-
10/17	1	1
10/18	1	1
10/19	-	-
10/20	1	1
10/23	2	2
10/24	-	-
10/25	-	-
10/26	2	2
11 days	9	9

Availability and Reliability

Within each area of system interest specific attributes must be listed and associated with functional categories. Each of these functional categories will probably have different availability requirements. It is obvious, for example, that the availability of a CPU is more important than that of a terminal, a system control program is more vital than a language component, and a language specification is more important than a primer.

The total system facilities viewed as an integral source of given capabilities may be categorized both according to the responsibility of the user and to the job to be done. Hardware, software, communications, and operational reasons have an impact on systems availability.

Availability is the probability that a system is running at any point during scheduled time. It is calculated as follows:

$$\text{Percent availability} = 100 \times \frac{\text{System usage time (uptime)}}{\text{Scheduled time}}$$

$$\text{Uptime} = \text{Scheduled time} - \text{system downtime}$$

Reliability is the probability that a system will give satisfactory performance—for a pre-established period of time—under operational and environmental conditions defined in advance. It is calculated as follows:

$$R = e^{t/T}$$

Here, $\bar{T}$ is the mean time between failures, and t the time over which a system is expected to operate. However, many computer centers prefer to use the following calculation:

$$R = \frac{\text{System usage time}}{\Sigma \text{ of interruptions}}$$

Reliability may also be defined as the extent to which a system or component performs its specified functions without any failures visible to the user.

Availability and reliability regard the system running at any point during scheduled time, and must be examined and ensured within a life cycle perspective. As such, they also define the extent to which the system (all components of hardware, software, and documentation provided by the supplier) may be depended upon to supply complete, correct results when required, given any combination of inputs. Any combination of inputs includes the certainty that the system will be presented and inputs are defined as invalid. Complete, correct results require detection, rejection, and error publication.

Availability and reliability require the timely and accurate provision of services and rest on system and design characteristics incorporated at the drafting stage.

Maintainability is the extend to which preventive maintenance can be performed without degrading availability.

Repairability is the speed with which a component failure can be detected and fully corrected.

After correction of a component failure, recoverability is the speed with which system facilities can be restored, including necessary correction of data damaged as a result of the failure.

Life cycle reliability has practical, easily defined service aspects. A system or component performs its specified functions without any failure visible to the user. The most important thing that can be said about hardware reliability (as, indeed, all other kinds of reliability) is that the basic design must be aimed initially at reliability, otherwise little reliability will be achieved. The question must be asked, Do we know that this can be done and be reliable? If not, such a product should either not be produced or labeled frankly as experimental.

The most obvious place to look for increased reliability in hardware is in the type of components employed in the design. Component and circuit reliability for some parts of the computer has increased through the years as computers have progressed from vacuum tubes to transistors to solid-state logic technology and beyond. Each of these advances has resulted in circuitry with a longer life between failures, which gives more consistent results throughout the life of the system. As dependence on on-line systems grows and the penalties for unavailability become more severe, it is evident that new approaches must be used relative to the reliability of hardware components.

Failing components must generally be self-repairing or self-replacing if they impact critical applications. If we are expected to entrust data to a computerized data base, we must be assured that the data will be available easily to authorized users, secure from unauthorized users, and secure from accidental or malicious destruction. This implies larger, faster, and more inexpensive direct access for on-line storage of the data base as well as higher reliability to avoid the problem of "lost" data, bad tracks, head crashes, and so on.

Reliability standards must be established for each machine, based on the expected failure rate of its components, and for each function, based on its criticality to the application of the user. Any specific on-line system can be designed with a predictable rate once the failure rate of its components is known. It is possible to build a computer system that will never fail completely, that is, it will always be usable even though some parts of it may be undergoing repair at any given time.

It is necessary, then, to analyze the use of each specific machine and establish a particular standard of reliability for that single piece of equipment. Means for the measurement of performance are essential to support the expected fail-soft techniques. It should be possible to tell at a glance which machines are functioning at full capacity, which at partial, and which are down. On those machines working at only a partial capacity, it should be possible to tell from the measurement which functions are impaired and what must be done to correct them. Simulators should also be designed to measure the effect on availability when a particular machine is removed from the system, either partially or wholly.

Availability of statistics regarding reliability experience is essential to users for the configuartion of reliable on-line systems to meet application requirements. The modeling and evaluation of reliability requires detailed quantitative data regarding failure experience and design objectives, coupled with detailed knowledge of impact on the applications of each failure condition. The data should include the mean failure and repair times and distribution characteristics by individual component, with categorization by secondary damage characteristic (e.g., data damaged or not damaged).

The detection of failures is critical and must take place as soon as possible after the failure occurs. The detection system may consist of hardware, software, or some combination, but it must be designed before the system is built so that it can take into account all of the design decisions which are made. Failure detection must be immediate and complete.

The detection mechanism should include a means for diagnosing the failure and isolating it to a specific machine, functional block, or component. It should attempt to pinpoint the failure as precisely as possible to make future maintenance simpler. The detection mechanism should immediately store the failure in the data base and external media. The data base storage is for future reference by the maintenance specialist and should note the time of the failure, the type of failure, the hardware location, the application being processed through the failing area, and any remedial action which was taken by the system or the system support. At the same time the error is logged, an alarm must be given to the operator to inform him that a failure has occurred. The combination of this alarm and the log will enable appropriate external action to be taken.

The system should then initiate internal correction, if at all possible. This may consist of switching in a redundant component in place of the failing component, bypassing the failing component while continuing to process with the remaining parts of the machine, dynamic reconfiguration of all the machines, or any other action made possible by the system's architecture. In general, this action should allow maximum use of the total system while the damaged components are repaired and replaced by external means.

Statistics should be kept on all failures for later analysis to determine if particular components are more susceptible to failure than others. A log of intermittent failures might also be used to determine the progressive weakening of a given component and thus permit its replacement before a failure occurs.

Particular consideration should be given to protective design which will make the system more independent of the environment, particularly in the areas of power, temperature, humidity, static electricity, impact, damage, and cleanliness. The same is true for the capability of implementing on-line maintenance; see Figure 13.1.

Let us summarize what has just been said. Improving service and enhancing actual system performance are worthwhile goals to be followed actively by keeping

Figure 13.1

On-line maintenance. The test is performed on the line, modem, DTE, environment

LOOP-BACK

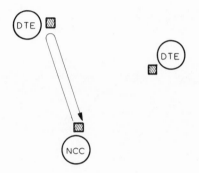

failure statistics and providing special units for telediagnostics and telecontrol. In brief, this means providing an on-line maintenance capability to assist the user. With downline loading and upline dumping facilities, the user can send messages and test the different modems by comparing the answer received to the signal. Further, diagnostics at the user's level allow screening for failures, localizing them, and calling for maintenance on a documented basis.

A data base must be organized so that it is able to give MTBI, MTBSI, MTTR, and MTOSI for each piece of equipment, with classification by type of failure. To ease corrective action interactive approaches should be used, plus a printing exception routine for a given connection, for instance, a connection which had more than five failures in a month.

Software Reliability

For over a quarter of a century computer software has been an adventure rather than serious, planned, and thoroughly controlled work. Many large system programming projects emerged as running propositions, but few have met goals, schedules, budgets, or prerequisites.

The objective should be to make software at least as reliable as hardware, especially in view of typical software repair times. Much more emphasis should be

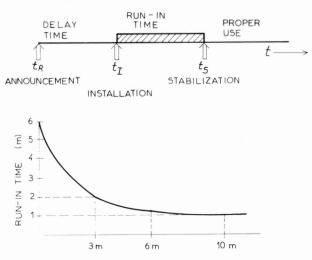

Figure 13.2
(a) Manufacturer's learning curve with a new software release;
(b) Installation takes place at client's site _x_ months after the announcement

placed on designing for prevention of failure, rather than repair, because of long repair times and the possible severe impact on the user's business operation. Certain applications will be so critical that no software failure can be tolerated, whereas others would be able to withstand some failure. One solution would be two sets of software: one that is very reliable, seldom changing, and with sufficient features to do a job but with no complexities, and the other a more complex, generalized type commonly used today.

Good initial system design, implementation, and testing are of paramount importance. The goal should be that software features will not be approved unless the designer can describe exactly how they may be tested out 100 percent. The specific limits must be tested and made known to the users.

Systems analysis and design must be done defensively, that is, the designer must assume that the worst will happen, invalid data will be presented to the system, unplanned use will occur, and modifications will need to be made. These factors, if accounted for in the initial design, will increase the overall reliability of the software.

Programs must be designed and implemented in a modular fashion—modular by end use, as seen by the user. In the future, when the software becomes a part of the hardware, this concept will be essential. In addition, the modules should be further broken down into small, relatively independent packets. When a failure occurs in software residing in the hardware, it must be possible to remove and replace only the failing portion, with other work continuing to run if it does not require the failing section.

When components are kept at the simplest possible level, changes may be isolated to a few specific components, and, by use of a standard software interface, these components may be replaced easily. Software simplicity helps not only the user but also the manufacturer and his representatives.

Figure 13.2 identifies three milestones: delay time, between announcement and installation, run-in time, between installation and stabilization, and proper use of the manufacturer's new software release. The learning curve of the manufacturer himself is significant and, along with him, that of the client. The run-in time varies from 1 to 6 months, depending on which point in the manufacturer's learning curve the installation at the client's site takes place.

Software design is another important factor affecting overall performance. Each software module should begin with a routine which validates all data input to it. All data entering the system should be checked; errors capable of stopping the software should be trapped. Processing of that data should be discontinued and an appropriate error message written. The emphasis here is on the prevention of software failures. Errors must be detected, isolated, diagnosed, published, and corrected. The design philosophy must be to catch errors early enough in processing logic to prevent or localize the damage caused by them.

When an error has been detected, it should be logged immediately. The user should have the ability to route a notification to the appropriate person, who is almost never the computer operator. With a good message and a log of the failure, this person can diagnose the problem and take corrective action. The criterion for a message to be "good" is if the user can know from this message the exact cause of the failure. Conversely, a message listing three possible causes is not a "good" message.

Other problems with software are operational. Considerable setup time is lost with some routines. In addition, it is sometimes necessary to consume further setup time if a scheduled interruption or failure has occurred and the operators must restart from a checkpoint. Lengthy setup time is certainly inconsistent with the concept of having an on-line system. Only by considering the total system requirements can ways be found to reduce total system setup time to a reasonable amount. Techniques such as overlapping the setup functions instead of having them end-to-end and eliminating others by storing results of previous setups offer some solutions.

Generally, one of the more serious losses of availability is the time required to set up and tear down computing facilities before and after production uses and time out. While the nature of the problem is such that this factor can probably never be reduced to zero, attention should be paid to lowering this major loss of available time.

Operator experience affects significantly both setup and the overall time needed to study the system. Figure 13.3 makes the distinction between experienced and inexperienced operators. Either case is subject to equipment variants, but the

Figure 13.3

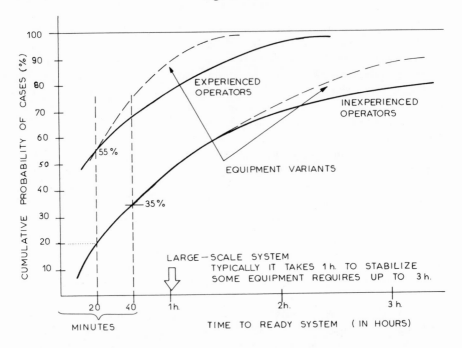

cumulative distribution of cases indicates that the probability is 55 percent for experienced operators versus 20 percent for inexperienced ones to prepare the system within 20 minutes. Further still, experienced operators will, in nearly all cases, prepare the system in less than 2 hours. This happens only in 70 percent of the cases for the less experienced. Evidently, such variations have a great impact on the downtime due to all causes.

A part is also played by how well the programs have been written and how many checkpoints are included to avoid total rerun of programs in the case of timeout. Figure 13.4 illustrates this by distinguishing dump time, recovery time, and total downtime due to all causes.

If we include in total recovery system restart, reconfiguration (if any), restore, reload, and rerun, then on the average

$$\frac{\text{Recovery}}{\text{Total system downtime (TSDT)}} = 36\%$$

$$\frac{\text{Dump time}}{\text{TSDT}} = 7\%$$

The dump time precedes recovery. If the system hangs up, we must dump it. And

$$\frac{\text{DT} + \text{R}}{\text{TSDT}} = 43\%$$

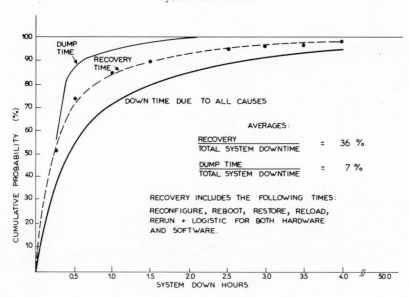

Figure 13.4
System downtime

However, some dump may go on simultaneously with recovery, so there is altogether a 40 percent increase over the loss of production time over the MTTR and MSDT factors we will be considering. Figure 13.5 further exemplifies the total system downtime.

The difference between total system interruption versus time of repair is demonstrated clearly. Short hardware interruptions are overwhelmed by the impact of the "other" factors affecting timeout. Indeed, software reasons, system stabilization, operator reasons, dumps, recovery, and the like all represent in this case a high multiple of the hardware downtime. Proportionally speaking, the impact of these factors is felt less in the case of long hardware interruptions. The average in a sample of installations of hardware interruptions over total system downtime was found to be 56 percent. Other significant findings indicated that in nearly 50 percent of the interruptions, the system was down for 0.5 hours or less. This 50 percent of all causes includes only 12 percent of hardware causes. Hence, in the lower end of the interruptions spectrum, 1/8 of the time-out reasons are due to hardware, while the other 7/8 are other causes. This is a significant finding in regard to system reliability.

Portability

The ease of being able to move a given product is becoming increasingly important as computer systems become larger and larger, either as central resources or as networks. Change and increasing movement are typical of today's needs, and this

Figure 13.5

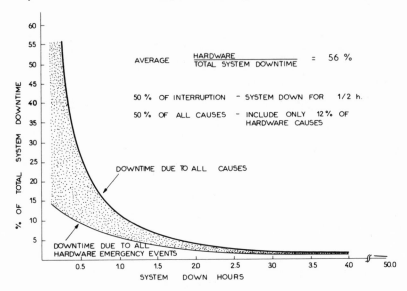

trend is expected to continue in the future. As computer systems become more interwoven into every phase of a company's business, hardware and software portability will affect every operation of the firm. The goal should be to make all hardware components easy to move from one place to another (similar to the way disc drives can be moved today) so that the maximum possible flexibility is attained.

Although this is just as true of software, one of the major problems with software is that it is not readily movable. Most appears to be designed on the assumption that only one machine will ever be utilized in any given company. It is very difficult to move libraries from one machine to another, and maintaining duplicate libraries is extremely difficult to do in a multimachine shop.

Software design, then, should permit one machine to adequately, fully, and easily back up another machine in the sense that any program normally run on machine A can be run on machine B without stopping machine B, without performing special setup, and without spending a fortune developing procedures and supplementary software. This need for smooth movement also includes possible movement between machines with differing configuration parameters, such as memory size, mass devices, and so on.

If the designer solves the problem of being able to move each component, it is fairly obvious that total system mobility has also been solved. An additional problem which may result from moving the total system, however, is the related environmental factors such as air conditioning, water supplies, and power supplies. Figure 13.6 illustrates the impact of power outages due to snowstorms, ice, and electrical storms. Similar graphs may be plotted for interruptions due to temperature variations and other environmental issues.

Figure 13.6

Impact of power outage on a system (Sample size: 200. Average system downtime due to power outage = 2.3 hours)

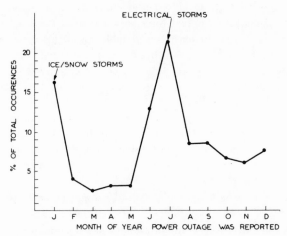

A crucial factor affecting portability is the need for conversions, both software and hardware. Conversions have been almost a way of life in the computer industry. Because of the typically small number of programs one had years ago and the fact that a number of the conversions were limited to hardware items, such as tape drives at a different density, the problems of conversion and the loss of available time due to conversions were fairly modest (or obscured). However, conversions now result in major losses of availability, and the trend appears to be getting even worse.

By way of illustration, consider a fair-sized company approaching 100,000 source modules (programs) during the late 1970s and early '80s: A simple conversion is needed; in fact, it is so simple that it takes only ten minutes of machine time and four hours of programmer time per source module. In total, it requires approximately 1,600 hours of computer time and 200 man-years of programming effort. Such numbers do not appear at all unreasonable to expect. Even fairly small installations will undoubtedly number source modules in the thousands. Clearly, there is a need for a system which will permit the industry to go forward at a reasonable pace of technological advance, and this system must therefore permit conversion to the advanced technology quickly and easily.

Conversion to new hardware is becoming increasingly complex as the number of data files and programs grows. Converting from one hardware to another becomes almost a traumatic experience with the hardware and software systems as currently designed. Users with libraries of thousands of tapes find that a tape conversion can cost thousands of hours of computer time. Disc conversions are unnecessarily cumbersome and timeconsuming. Conversion to take full advantage of increased memory size can cost a small fortune.

The concept of conversion is applicable, in varying degrees, as one changes the configuration of the computing facilities complex in any way—adding or subtracting, memory, hardware devices, new or revised software components, and so on. The impact of such changes on the availability of uninvolved system facilities should be minimal.

We are all familiar with possible partial solutions, such as data independence and correctly designed and applied high level languages. Special hardware conversion devices also appear to have considerable merit, for instance, a hardware device capable of transferring all data from one disc methodology to another in a matter of seconds. Conversion over time—a common approach using emulators and dual-density devices—does not appear to be adequate to meet today's real needs, let alone those of the 1980s.

The goal of conversion to new hardware should be to provide a smooth and economical conversion method for each class of hardware, including terminals, memory, tapes, discs, and printers. Furthermore, full advantage should be taken of the new components, instead of merely running just as one would under the old methodology.

Conversion of software is particularly troublesome. Relatively simple changes, such as a new version of a compiler or the installation of a new release of an operating system, are decisions of major proportion to a company performing many different types of computing covering thousands of programs, many of which are operating in real time. Figure 13.7 illustrates this by presenting the mean time of system interrupt as a function of hardware, software, and operational reasons. The reader will appreciate that the low points in MTOSI are due to new software releases and new hardware features. The high points, good availability, identify improvements in MTOSI as the system matures. However, because of new software releases and hardware features, such improvements do not last long. This definition considers the system either up or down. In addition there is "downgrading."

Statistics show that for 90 percent of the occurrences when a peripheral unit (new or old) interrupts the system, the system as a whole, or parts thereof, will be out of service for several hours. This is very important for on-line systems. Statistics document that even if the repair of a given terminal or other peripheral takes one hour, on the average a peripheral will be *out* for 6½ hours more because the maintenance service is not informed on time, the software people do not know how to handle a new problem, and the common carrier is overloaded or subject to failures of aging equipment. Essentially, this means that for remote peripherals, we should add the risk of line interrupt.

A great deal more can be done to build longevity and flexibility into better software and hardware. The central computer resources may be buffered through front ends. Software may be designed with storage parameters which can be varied to take advantage of additional main storage when it is available.

Particular attention is also necessary in the area of data conversion. Technological advances, or simply changes in operating systems are accompanied by changes in format, access methods, etc., so that files created on the old system cannot be read on the new system. A simple conversion tool, capable of transforming the old files with minimum overhead, should be part of the new system facilities.

Figure 13.7
Impact of software conversion on a large-scale system (average MTBSI = 80 hours)

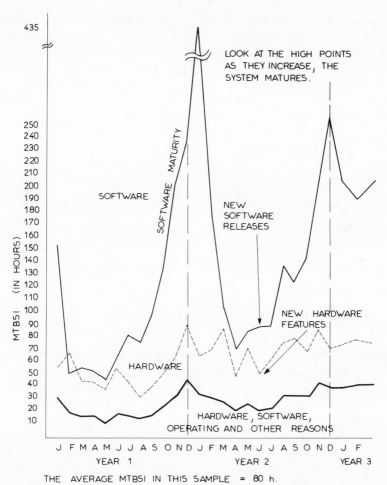

Further, the conversion of documentation still needs a simple solution. This applies to both hardware and software, but primarily to the impact on application documentation. The documentation for an application program must often be changed substantially when a new compiler is utilized or new discs are installed. Ideally, some automatic system should be offered which would produce operating and programming documentation. This automatic system would operate on computer documentation files to convert their data to the new methodology, and a subsequent printout run would automatically produce the desired new documentation. Operating and programming documentation should describe tapes and discs to be mounted, estimated running time, the sort to be used, flowcharts, record structure layouts, and so on. Computer-assisted automatic methodology should be developed so that documentation conversion can be done readily to support all hardware and software changes.

It is appropriate to add that total system conversion is simply not considered to be possible. Any replacement model should simply be an improved system which permits prior systems to coexist and run existing work, producing results identical to the previous system, with well thought out partial conversions as the only practical method of keeping technology advancing.

14

Systems Maintenance

Maintainability was one of the earliest preoccupations for the purpose of ensuring reliability. This issue is once again coming under scrutiny in regard to the life cycle considerations which we have presented. But many factors have changed. Maintainability has broadened, become more complex, and now demands a higher degree of expertise. With the multiplication of the terminals, new parameters enter the reliability equation.

Figure 14.1 gives an example of the growth of on-line systems. Two curves are plotted in terms of terminals installed over the years. They belong to two different industrial organizations, yet they exhibit the same trend.

Maintainability has to be looked at much more carefully now; crucial points where something could go wrong have multiplied. Computers must be used to assist in this task, otherwise the job will escape control. Furthermore, the reliability standards we need to establish should reflect fully the coming on-line requirements, such as electronic mail. The current standards have existed for twenty-five years. Twenty-five years hence it will be the twenty-first century.

Complex data communications networks will bring forward reliability and maintainability requirements beyond the current state of the art. Based on experience, we can only project what may be necessary in terms of availability and on-line maintenance capability through the establishment of a network control center. These subjects are treated here to help establish standards for the work done at the various data communications centers of computer manufacturers and user organizations.

Time of Systems Interrupt

The first phase of system maintainability concerns the extent to which preventive maintenance can be performed without degrading availability.

Figure 14.1
Growth of on-line systems

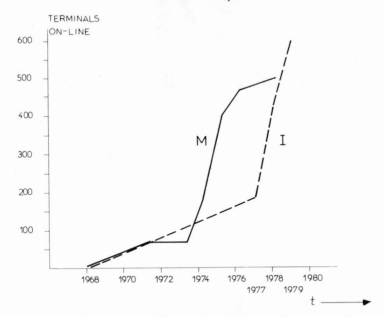

The second, called repairability, is the speed with which a component failure can be detected and fully corrected. The measurement used is mean time to repair, but this as stated, is not sufficient. Reference has been made already to recoverability and to mean time of system interrupt as the objective means for measuring system interrupt. Figure 14.2 presents the distinctions between these factors. Each element of MTTR and of MTOSI is indicated clearly.

Delays due to MTTR are presented in Table 14.1. Within a twenty-day period, such delays accounted for 2.421 minutes. Sixty telephone calls had to be placed over that period (an average of three per day) to pressure the field maintenance into minimizing the timeout. This is characteristic of sites with 'repeated failure records—hence, the wisdom of a well-organized preventive maintenance program. Although preventive maintenance has been associated with hardware since the first generation of computers, most users would agree that it has a much more drastic effect on availability today than in previous times.

The preventive maintenance required for the numerous kinds of components varies widely, depending upon the component. A unit without moving mechanical parts, such as today's typical semiconductor memories, needs preventive mainte-nance far less than a mechanical unit with moving parts, such as a disc drive.

But the first requirement for proper maintenance of hardware is that the component be designed for preventive maintenance. There must be such simple provisions as accessibility of the units, handles on removable units, doors that swing

Figure 14.2
Mean time of system interruption and mean time to repair

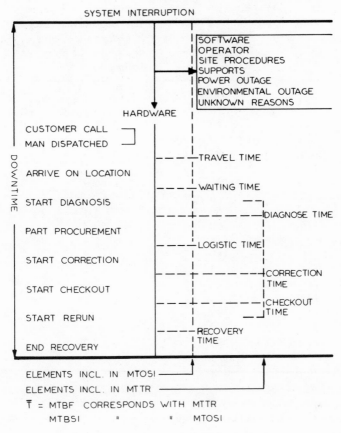

wide enough to allow access to all components, limited exposure to electrical shock, and so on. If an engineer has to assume some impossible position in order to check or remove a component, the chance of preventive maintenance being performed well is reduced.

Another basic requirement is that the entire computer system not be stopped. The concept of varying components off-line for preventive maintenance must be carried further than it is today. Standard interfaces for all components are a must for quick changing of failing parts or the immediate isolation of problems. Such standardization will eliminate many current practices detracting from availability, such as requiring an hour to replace a console typewriter. This capability will also facilitate the addition of new components without stopping the whole machine.

With on-line systems, there is also the problem of interfacing with the telephone company's equipment.

Table 14.1
Delays in Repair of Terminal Failures

Date	Elapsed time in minutes (MTTR)	Telephone Calls Made to Center that Same day to Signal the Failure
10/23	250	1
10/24	260	1
10/25	10	1
10/26	75	1
10/27	81	4
10/30	150	3
10/31	123	4
11/2	30	1
11/3	69	1
11/6	60	3
11/7	118	4
11/8	342	3
11/9	86	6
11/10	36	2
11/13	108	3
11/14	233	11
11/15	150	6
11/16	35	2
11/17	175	3
20 days	2.421 minutes	60

Getting cooperation between engineers on such simple items as coordinating preventive maintenance can be beneficial to the user. But it is handicapped by the lack of standards in the area of preventive maintenance in terms of the amount of time and frequency with which it should be performed on each component. Another crucial issue is the production of a feedback reporting system.

The information systems manager should know what preventive maintenance is being performed on each computer component, and measure this against the degree of reliability. The system should maintain a log of component malfunctions that would pinpoint units needing additional preventive maintenance. An example of this is the type of log that is now maintained for input–output errors. By examining such a log on each component, the engineers could identify those units that were malfunctioning more frequently than designed to. Diagnostic routines must be able to run in the normal job stream without disrupting the entire system. This permits testing to see if a component is failing and to check a newly installed component. The diagnostic routine used in preventive maintenance should also specify which component in a series is failing; an example is when there is a problem in a terminal modem or communication line and the failing component needs to be isolated.

Preventive maintenance of software, for all practical purposes, does not exist. This situation must be corrected. Basic to this is the requirement that software maintenance personnel install changes to correct problems before they are manifested in a catastrophic way. This is not being done, since these people are trained not to install a change until a bad experience occurs with the problem.

Other crucial problems are the slow response to reported problems and the poor condition of the system delivered. Since software does not deteriorate through use as does hardware, if it were delivered in reliable working condition there would not be any need for preventive maintenance.

Preventive Maintenance

To facilitate preventive maintenance software must be constructed in a logical building block process with audit trails left by each component. (Many problems in software are difficult to find because as modules pass data between them, such simple rules as checking condition codes are not followed.)

Further, preventive maintenance of software implies continued testing of the product at the supplier's site, since all copies delivered to users are exact replicas of the end item produced, not similar copies to be continually tested in the field for conformance with the master copy as is the case with hardware. Today's concepts of product testing and integration testing must be extended indefinitely beyond the initial release date. Test scenarios must be expanded continually with more rigorous tests, both devised by the producer's test designers and derived from faults exposed in user installations. Fixes to software problems should become available to user personnel so that decisions can be made to apply a fix to the system prior to the error actually occurring. Fixes should also be tied more closely to logical modules and documentation more clearly describe the problem they fix. Test routines should be available to test whether the fix is operating properly. This is just as essential with software as it is with hardware, yet it is almost totally unavailable. Stated differently, more emphasis is needed in software design and development on principles similar to those used in providing maintainability in hardware.

It is not unusual to find that a failure in a new function added to a software package causes failures in functions that worked satisfactorily on earlier versions. Increased modularity of design would help insulate proven components from changes in other components. An insistence upon standard interfaces would allow substitution of components with similar functions when a new component fails. However, this is not the case, as Figure 14.3 points out. Statistics reported by a major airline clearly demonstrate how, every time a new application is introduced into the real-time system, there is a sharp drop in mean time of system interrupt. Notice that recovery of the earlier MTOSI level is not linear. This seesaw curve identifies the trial and error approach often used to fix software failures.

Measurement of software failures must be done in the same careful way as for hardware failures. On the average, the number of failures due to software exceeds those due to hardware in most installations. It is essential that one is aware of the

Figure 14.3
Introduction of a new application causes a drop in MTOSI

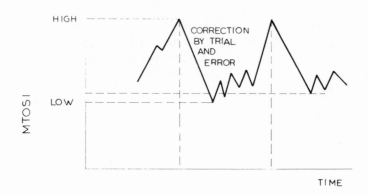

number of system failures that may be expected and the amount of time to recover or return the system to full operation when a failure occurs.

Finally, the application of preventive maintenance to documentation is more akin to software than to hardware. There is also a need for continued testing of the documentation at the supplier's site aimed at better satisfying the requirements for usability, accuracy, completeness, and currency.

Since documentation is not an independent end item but must at all times reflect an exact correspondence with, or representation of, an end product (hardware or software), it must be changed whenever the corresponding facility is changed. Thus, even if documentation were issued in the best condition and there were no need (which there is) to test for outright errors, omissions, and, ambiguous and misleading statements, there would still be a need to make changes in documentation in order to keep it current.

Above all, documentation should be organized to facilitate the diagnosing of problems. Options should be available for transmission of documentation in machine-sensible form for hard-copy or soft-copy replication by the user, as desired, and for access from a central store via remote terminals.

In conclusion, maintenance of the total system depends on the maintenance of software, hardware, and documentation. Total system dependability is not possible without each of these components, and they must all have preventive maintenance at a level that meets the requirements of the total system.

For every basic component we mentioned, maintainability may be expressed in mean time per maintenance action, MTMA. The critical variables to be included—troubleshooting, testing, locating—all relate directly to preventive maintenance.

The effectiveness of the maintenance effort is a direct function of the training of the field engineers in doing their job the best way possible; often this is a long and tedious process. As Figure 14.4 documents, there is a big difference between MTBF and MTTR as functions of maintenance know-how. Reliability never really reaches

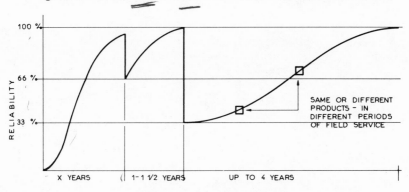

Figure 14.4
A big difference in MTBF and MTTR is in maintenance know-how

100 percent; it takes years in research and development to get an acceptable level. The product is transferred to manufacturing—and there is a major reliability drop. It takes 1 to 1.5 years to stretch matters out at the production floor. But it takes up to 4 years to fine-tune the field maintenance. The drop in reliability right after a product is marketed can be of appreciable proportion.

Perspectives in Repairability

The cost of maintenance, whether for systematic (preventive) or repair operations, is steadily on the increase. Such cost is very much influenced by two factors—personnel and spares—roughly in a 2:1 ratio.

Traditionally, there has been a certain ratio between the yearly cost of maintenance and the total equipment cost for computers. Figure 14.5 identifies the findings of a research project. Equipment from different manufacturers ranges from $100,000 to $1 million. The percent of sales price varies from 4.50 to 6.8 within this bracket. For minicomputers below the $100,000 level, it can go to 8 percent and beyond. This money is paid to the computer manufacturer (or specialized maintenance firm) for system maintenance and for handling efficiently the problems of equipment repair.

We defined repairability as the speed with which a component failure is detected and fully corrected. To any computer user, repairability obviously is one of the more important factors affecting the total system availability concept. The sooner the malfunctioning component—hardware, software, or documentation—can be detected and fully corrected, the sooner recovery of system facilities can take place to meet the user's requirements. Hardware repair is the most clear-cut concept with respect to computer system availability. However, without valid statistics it becomes an inefficient task.

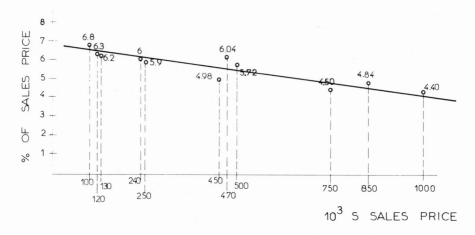

Figure 14.5
Maintenance cost as a function of sales price

Depending upon the application, the effects of a malfunctioning system range from a simple temporary delay to the creation of catastrophic conditions. Many on-line real-time applications are provided with a backup because of an urgent need to have the system in operation at all times. It is anticipated that future computers will be built with componnents designed for greatly increased reliability. A component failure will be detected easily through the use of improved diagnostic equipment and software facilities.

Diagnostic Centers

Repairability can be enhanced through steady, well-done preventive maintenance. Some computer manufacturers stipulate that they will inspect equipment to see that it works correctly before agreeing to put the equipment on a maintenance contract. The policies of other manufacturers provide for maintenance, but an overhaul, if needed, will be charged to the customer. Policies may stipulate payments on an hourly service rate or a flat rate, or still others may contain general statements to the effect that the manufacturer's first obligation is to support its direct customers before extending such efforts to others.

But the best solution for users is not to be as dependent as they are today upon the availability of the supplier's service personnel to diagnose and repair hardware malfunctions. With improved and simplified diagnostic facilities, plus basic training in the use of these tools, the user's personnel should be able to determine whether or not the malfunction may be repaired without the assistance of the supplier. In those cases where only a simple replacement is necessary, the user should be able to perform the repair. This self-service concept may be accomplished through improved design of components and better diagnostic tools.

A diagnostic plan is most important. Statistics, error messages, oscilloscopes, and so on, are expensive adornments unless there is a rational way to synthesize symptoms and employ the techniques to discover the problem. Once the error has been localized to a component, it should be repairable off-line or it should be possible to connect the device remotely to a diagnostic center.

Diagnostic centers allow centralization of specialized diagnostic expertise (on-line maintenance capability). The techniques required are not novel, since the problem is similar to data flow from tape drives to controllers to channels to switching buses to memory. The distinction with teleprocessing is that other suppliers are involved and integrated test procedures are required.

Measurements are important and so is the steady and comprehensive recording of measurements. Operating statistics enable both suppliers and users to evaluate the personnel involved in repair, the repair procedures that are provided, and the efficiency of the diagnostic facilities.

Software repairability must be viewed from two perspectives: supplier-developed programs and user-developed application programs.

With supplier-developed programs the user finds frequently that the programs do not meet the claims made for them, that they give meaningless error responses that bugs and fixes have not been disseminated to them soon enough to preclude the waste of precious hours or days trying to solve problems for which others have discovered solutions earlier. Software is rarely designed for quick repair. Substantial research effort is needed to develop methodologies which ensure repair quickly.

In user-developed application programs, much available time is lost because the user simply is not sure whether the basic software or the program is at fault. To help correct this, it is important that the software both protect itself and publish clear messages in the event of malfunction or improper use.

Improved design of diagnostics is an important factor in software repairability. Currently, programmers may use only software debugging facilities, and a special software process must be employed to implement the facilities. Some simple means must be found to switch to diagnostic mode, perhaps by hardware.

As in hardware, the measurement used in software repairability is the mean time to repair. It addition, there should be measures showing the nature of the failures in order to improve training of personnel, maintain tighter control over program development and debugging processes, and reduce the requirement for software repairs. In determining the cost of a failure, the time required to make a repair is as important as the frequency of failure.

Repairability of the total system reflects all the problems and solutions discussed above under hardware and software. Often, the point of total system repairability is to isolate the cause of the malfunction.

The mean downtime (or time of system interrupt, MTOSI) includes fault finding, removal, repair, supply actions, reinstallation checking, checking of software, program reruns, recovery, dumps, and restart. The operational availability can be calculated by the following algorithm:

$$\text{Operational availability } = \frac{\text{MTBF}}{\text{MTBF } + \text{ MTOSI}}$$

Do-It-Yourself Maintenance

We said that the best solution for users is not to depend—at least not exclusively—on the manufacturer or outside maintenance service. To accomplish the self-service concept in hardware repairability the supplier and the users must predetermine the standards and criteria under which the users may perform self-maintenance. Furthermore, as is advisable in all cases, detailed records of occurrences must be kept for the manufacturer, who should contstantly review this program and improve upon it.

Preventive self-maintenance and repair can be best implemented through an on-line connection to the manufacturer. The remote site operator (user's own field engineer) must be able to do both on-line inquiry and batch data entry. In one application for on-line inquiry, the operator uses an IBM 3275 under CICS software. For batch data, such as transactions to update the master file, the operator keys in the transaction to the central system where it is accumulated on the disc. For support purposes to the user, the manufacturer's maintenance service—and other authorized remote stations—can do inquiries against the maintenance data base through terminals.

Here is how one organization related its experience to the manufacturer-provided maintenance, and the solution its followed afterward. During the first six months the system was used to create new system software, modify existing system software, and work on internal projects. We learned that the response time of the repairman of the company with which we were dealing was between one-half to two working days. We felt that the maintenance contract was not being taken seriously; effective trouble-shooting was not started before 10 A.M. and rarely extended beyond 3 P.M.. In addition, if we were unfortunate enough to tell the field service representative that a repair was not immediately required (such as a magnetic tape giving parity errors), then it was never fixed.

Observing that we could not change the spirit of the field service, our next step was to try to find an alternative. First we asked that regular checks be made on the system. We discovered that no preventive maintenance whatsoever was included in the contract and that if we wanted it we had to pay extra for it—even though we were paying nearly $20,000 a year for "maintenance services"! Talks with the vendor led to a proposal stipulating that each week a repairman would run some tests for a fixed monthly cost. However, nothing in the proposal even mentioned which tests were to be run or for how long. That is how we decided to get involved ourselves.

We noticed that the first thing that the repairman did on coming was to run reliability tests to see if any anomalies could be detected. We found that we could do this easily. With no more background than that, we established a procedure whereby we would run overnight tests every week in the following rotation:

Memory	week 1
CPU	week 2
Discs	week 3

The reason for choosing the above tests was that an undetected fault originating in the memory, the CPU, or during the transfer of information to or from a disc had a good chance of becoming catastrophic for the system. This is the kind of fault we were after.

Faults originating from the card reader, the line printer, or the magnetic tape units could be detected almost immediately. Therefore, we adopted a wait and see attitude for these parts of the system.

At any rate, after several months of operation we saw that most problems were due to faulty memory boards, not from electromechanical components. Once we localized a fault in the system, we then isolated the bad component or unit and, if possible, reconfigured the system in a degraded mode of operation. This allowed us to send the bad component for repair, wait until it came back, and reinsert it in the system. We thought that with this solution we could benefit from having a stock of repaired and adjusted parts, but were reluctant to jump all the way into doing our own work.

By the time we developed do-it-yourself capabilities, we were almost at the end of our original maintenance contract and not ready to extend it. Also, prices had gone up. We were told that our original maintenance contract had been setup at two-year-old prices and that this year the vendor was seriously considering an increase.

We decided, therefore, to shop around for suitable maintenance firms willing to troubleshoot our equipment on an on-call basis. This solution promised to be much cheaper than the full parts and labor maintenance contract, and—given the experience we had been accumulating—it could be tried without risk. Suddenly we were maintenance people. The cyclic tests run on memory, CPU, and discs made us somewhat confident that the system would be fairly reliable.

Of course, the worst can always happen, such as an undetected bug which turns out to be uninterpretable by our diagnostics. The time required to diagnose an intermittent fault is potentially very long, but it would be for the outside serviceman as well. It was our experience that the first indication of a fault of any kind is the progressive destruction of the system software residing on disc. So as soon as we suspect something is getting worse, we re-create a system disc. (The re-creation of a user disc takes much longer, from one to two hours for a three-quarters full disc. However, this procedure is rarely necessary since we separated the user disc files from the system disc after noticing that the user disc rarely gets scratched.) Should a disc, or a processor, go down completely, we can load data onto the other disc and/or operate with a single processor. The possibility of the whole system going down at once is rather remote.

Once in a great while we faced a problem we were unable to trace to the hardware, operating system, software, or to the foreground/background method of operation. In these cases, if the problem does not disappear it soon becomes apparent if the hardware is at fault. If the hardware has a bug, it is certain to get worse; that may not be much of a diagnostic method, but it works.

We soon learned how sensitive computer systems are to temperature and to variations in temperature. A good way to prevent or postpone potential problems is to make sure that the ambient temperature of the computer room is constant and slightly cool. Regular checks should be made of the air circulation inside the racks in the area where there is a great deal of heat dissipation.

Another diagnostic tool we used is the test job. From time to time we run a few jobs which seem to exercise most of the software and hardware, then compare their output with known results.

Finally, we do send suspect memory boards to the manufacturer to be readjusted and margined.

These fairly simple procedures keep our system alive and well. If this method can be used for a central installation, why not for the DIS sites? Here supplier maintenance is often a complex issue, and the user has to be very careful with uptime and with keeping down the labor costs.

15

The Network Control Center

A primary cause of degradation and malfunction of a communications system is the environment. Concern for associated environmental factors is germaine to any electronic equipment.

Normally, the central computer site or the distributed host computers receive ample attention in this area. However, data communications systems which have distributed terminals, concentrators, and remote miniprocessors are commonly neglected. When the electronic devices are located at other than the central site, environmental concerns often do not receive the same priority of attention. Yet, distributed information systems require the same attention as the central installation.

Quite often the user is misled into this situation. To present a product in the most attractive manner to a prospective customer, the manufacturer makes statements such as, "it operates in a normal office environment," "no special installation needs," "just plug it in like a typewriter." As a result, the user thinks that the equipment has inherent immunity to its actual operating environment; in reality, it is highly susceptible to adverse environmental conditions. Figure 15.1 presents the total view of the user's relation to the physical and logical resources. The reason for studying, projecting, and implementing a network control center, NCC, lies in this fact and in the desire to provide automatic, not manual, control solutions.

Networks today involve hundreds of terminals. Projects are already under study for information systems with 3,000, 6,000, even 12,000 terminals. A thousand user-operated minicomputers will easily be involved in such network structures. From an overall service maintenance point of view, the network is only a component of an end-to-end customer service. Other components are the terminals, modems, network access channels, and so on. It is both unfeasible and inefficient to check such complex systems manually. The answer lies in the NCC, which is becoming a fundamental building block to achieving a division of responsibility.

185

Figure 15.1
User-oriented applications facility

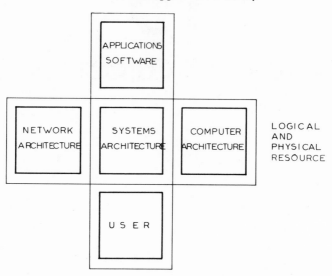

A basic, and very critical, issue for networks is never get out to diagnose; everything must be done on-line, whether it involves hard-level diagnostics, or a major part of the software. Also, the maintenance people should replace boards only when the client cannot do it. The object of NCC is the enhancement of these hardware and software engineering aims. A primary goal of design engineering is to produce a product that will function properly within set ranges of environmental conditions. Due to diverse topology and to operating conditions not always under control, the network architect cannot assume that conditions will vary over known ranges; actual conditions will occasionally exceed nominal ranges.

Major environmental factors include temperature and humidity which work together to attack electronic equipment; temperature is the more significant factor with today's component technology. Although not usually considered, dirt and dust particles can render subtle yet extensive damage to electronic equipment. In addition, there is primary power, proper installation, power stability, and power availability must be considered.

Environmental issues are not the only ones of a disturbing influence. Operational factors, too, contribute to equipment malfunctions, particularly, wrong operations and wear and tear. Furthermore, maintenance itself often leaves much to be desired in terms of performance. A study which we did at the General Electric/ Bull facility some years ago documented that one-third of the failures were hardware oriented, one-third had software reasons, and one-third were traced to prior intervention by the maintenance engineer. Notice, however, that the classic maintenance approach—undoubtedly influenced from the time of mechanical equipment—concerns itself with the wear and tear of the machine itself, hence, with hardware. Though still necessary, this concern is today inadequate.

Another reason for equipment failure is a combination of minor factors of which the most important is the impact of electrostatic effects on the magnetic recording media. We have had the experience of terminals with a cassette unit which does not register the transaction because of the electrostatic effect of the pavement. In another case, a cassette registered bit errors every time the nearby traffic lights changed.

A final cause behind equipment failure is quality histories (field operations and service) and the possibility of inference. The classic case is that quality records are nonexistent, incomplete, or written in a way which does not lend itself to extrapolation and inference. An NCC can correct this situation by offering the needed data base. The procedures and the streamlining required for the establishment of an NCC provide much more in terms of breadth and depth in the reorganization necessary for efficient, well-rounded maintenance operations.

Briefly, the benefits to be derived through on-line maintenance are the following:

1. Saves personnel.
2. Maintenance people become better acquainted with background and foreground failures.
3. Detailed planning reduces frustration for maintenance people and for users.
4. Provides for schedule changes as the need arises.
5. All spares are kept active, and boards are on continuous check-up.
6. Makes feasible a dynamic reconfiguration of the network.
7. Failure statistics are carefully maintained; examination and inference may be made on-line.
8. Hardware tracking is automated with a minimal use of the network for downline tests.

Environmental Factors

Adverse temperatures, as evidenced by extreme heat or cold, can cause a myriad of component weaknesses. All manufacturers specify an acceptable operating temperature range for their equipment, but most users consider operating temperatures as a factor only when the equipment is in use. They are not concerned with environmental temperatures when the equipment is dormant, such as during long night hours or weekends. However, just the fact that equipment is on creates the same susceptibility to temperature extremes as when it is functioning.

The mean time between failures for a given component will be reduced by 50 percent for every 10 degrees above the normal temperature.

The differential between room temperature and the temperature at the top of an electronic equipment cabinet is usually 10 to 15 degrees.

A minicomputer-based system with memory and associated electronics easily achieves a 15-to-20-degree differential. If that equipment is located in a room that on weekends reaches 95 to 100°F due to air conditioning shutdown, the cabinet temperature can approach 115 to 120°F.

Although not in use, the system's being powered leads to the same degradation and, eventually, permanent damage. This results in highly error-prone operation on Mondays and, ultimately, random and seemingly unrelated circuit failures. Users must be fully aware of all possible environmental extremes and either lower the equipment power or provide auxiliary air conditioning or heating equipment.

It is also important that a record of past temperature extremes be maintained, with room and cabinet temperatures monitored simultaneously. A temperature chart recorder should note all temperatures. Even inexpensive maximum-indicating thermometers are effective if read and reset on a frequent basis. Ideally, a temperature threshold alarm system for unattended equipment would alert personnel when preset temperature conditions are reached.

Humidity usually is not a major factor until condensation begins or the saturated air coupled with dirt and dust particles begins to exhibit a conductivity characteristic. However, continuing high humidity or interchanges of very humid and very dry conditions can create problems. At Washington State University* in the mid-sixties the maxicomputer exhibited effects of "silver migration," and it took three weeks of tests (and time out) to find the reasons and to correct them.

A high dirt or dust environment will first become evident in the filters located in the cabinet blowers. Frequent inspection and cleaning of these filters not only ensure that dirt and dust particles do not reach the electronic components, but also provides for free air flow through the equipment. If the internal air flow is impeded, the temperature differential will increase dramatically. A moderately dirty filter could easily raise the differential over 30 degrees.

Under extreme conditions, high humidity coupled with a dusty or dirty atmosphere can produce a conductive solution that condenses on electronic components, causing a component to literally destroy itself. For example, an electronic system that experienced chronic failures was found to have a virtually imperceptible coating of "dust" on each board. Isolation of equipment in a closed room with directly filtered air outlets or vents is ample precaution.

The environmental factor of primary power is another matter. The first concern here is correct grouping of the circuits, which is the most common cause of system malfunctions if done improperly. While this may seem self-evident, it is not unusual to find a significant potential existing between the primary power neutral lead and the actual frame ground. It is normally assumed that within a building's electrical distribution system this interconnection is properly maintained, yet in a

---

*Pullman, Washington. This is a point where the High Sierras of the Pacific Northwest and the Nevada Desert meet.

multistory building a significant difference can develop. For instance, in a given installation when a minicomputer's magnetic tape peripheral was turned off the minicomputer's memory of information was mutilated. In effect, the system was "floating," inviting any kind of spurious power signal to invade the primary system. The assumption that the primary power was properly terminated and would maintain that termination led to this failure.

Though every well designed power supply will compensate for nominal power fluctuations, it is not unusual to have relatively common power variations that exceed the tolerances of the equipment's power supplies. In such environments, auxiliary primary power regulation equipment—which is relatively low cost—should be installed at all sites having unattended or multiple device dependency such as remote concentrators or remote input–output processors. This level of precaution is usually not warranted at a remote interactive terminal, but it may be necessary to a remote job entry (RJE) terminal site.

If actual power outages are a reasonable, or even remote, probability, and the associated application's operational sensitivity is totally intolerant of such outages, an uninterruptible power supply (UPS) must be considered. Economic factors heavily influence a UPS decision. If a UPS is to be implemented, care should be taken to include all critical system equipment and devices.

Unfortunately, the impact of environmental factors is appreciated only after the damage has been done; in retrospect, the appropriate attention would have been relatively easy. A poor operating environment can reduce the finest designed equipment to valueless junk. Remote sensors, however, cannot handle everything. While a remote temperature system, for instance, integrates nicely with a network control center, humidity and power supply, not that easy to automate, call for inspection procedures. Tymnet, for example, has instituted teams with clear-cut missions for inspection at the client level. This involves the customer's premises in general and checks on humidity and power supply, as well as suggestions for the correction of power failures.

A Maintenance Architecture

Control of environmental factors and supervision of critical system components—terminals, hosts, concentrators, modems, access channels—and the network itself will be exercised by the network control center. It will operate as a test and repair center, responsible for the maintenance of all data services in the geographical area under its authority.

The basic maintenance architecture calls for this center to integrate physically the personnel involved in all aspects in its territory, and to provide the ability to centralize maintenance aspects effectively. This includes customer trouble reporting, testing, service implementation, and quality analysis of end-to-end customer data service. These four points summarize the advantages which on-line network maintenance offers. The end-to-end service is a prerequisite for all on-line systems.

Customer quality service starts with the logging of errors. It proceeds with error monitoring and analysis—the two pillars on which diagnostics rest. It is enhanced by the possibility of downline maintenance.

Both preventive (systematic) and failure maintenance may be assisted through automatic on-line procedures, for example, network supervisory activities, fault isolation, and maintenance dispatching. Maintenance dispatching minimizes the time required both for the location of spares and for the allocation of scarce, expensive maintenance personnel. In the Tymnet network control center, for instance, the optimization of maintenance personnel is done by specialization and by location. Inventory management is on the NCC computer. All spares are distributed; common spares attract particular attention.

For fail-soft purposes network reconfiguration is done on-line at the NCC by a simulator. The simulator projects possible solutions, and the chief maintenance engineer decides on the alternatives. Maintenance schedules are established one month in advance; schedule changes, as the need arises, are computer assisted. The scheduling of people, including addresses, etc., so that maintenance personnel can always be identified, is also done by computer. This level of detailed planning is explicit enough to give minimum trouble to the operations of the Tymnet network and of the subscribers.

The computer, though it can be of great assistance, cannot do everything. A well-planned understructure is necessary, and this involves procedural issues. At Datapac (Bell Canada), for instance, not only is the maintenance force dedicated to the network but it is upgraded and re-evaluated continually. The same is true of maintenance procedures. There is little paper orientation; all data is passed into memory and kept at the network control center for retrieval and examination.

Quality histories kept on a data base not only permit investigations by management, but allow the maintenance engineer to interrogate, examine, and run diagnostics before visiting the subscriber's premises. This is very important for the future development of on-line applications, their maintainability, and dependability. It is also a good means for cost reduction in the maintenance operation itself. Bell Canada has 2,000 men performing maintenance work. Computerization has brought a savings of 10 to 15 percent in personnel costs or between 200 and 300 men per year. Not only is this enough to pay for the on-line solution, but also service has improved greatly. The network control center is the "beyond the human capabilities" extension of the network supervisor. Maintenance dispatched from this center covers preventive maintenance coordination, fault isolation and repair dispatching, replacement schedules, and spare parts management. Reconfigurations are made on-line through a simulator as are inferences. Changes are made through cathode ray tube displays. Scheduled interventions are run on a computer and are made one month ahead of time. Failure statistics on all units are kept very carefully and demands on manufacturing are made accordingly.

The correction of power failures has been greatly assisted through this data base. Power failure reasons were found to be the single largest improvement in reliability. In one case, the node was on the same line with the elevator.

Figure 15.2
Datapac overall network maintenance architecture

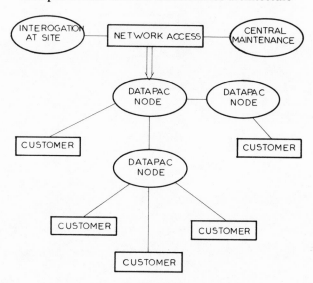

The next most important fact in improving reliability has been the tracking of failures to uncover their reason and dispatching accordingly by specialized personnel. However, at least one NCC found it necessary to discontinue hardware tracking; many signals were interpreted by the remote computers as commands (and the overhead was heavy).

Figure 15.2 identifies the overall network maintenance architecture at Datapac. The network control center organization is shown in Figure 15.3.

The computer-run data base includes quality statistics, failure rates by equipment and its components, and downline maintenance capabilities. Both the end equipment (terminals, concentrators, hosts) and the lines as well as the modems are part of this capability. Tymnet, which uses exclusively Bell System data sets, considers the modem and the line to be one in terms of maintenance responsibility.

The soft-copy interactive terminals which access the quality history data bases are given to clerks answering customers' demands, hardware/software analysts for correlation studies, maintenance supervisors, experts to conduct tests by way of instrumentation, and dispatchers (expediting the maintenance services).

The software answers key questions concerning all trouble within a given section (current and historical trends); the specific trouble in which sections are currently; trends analysis; and the current application and its historical trend.

The new generation of tests, in terms of systems, methods, and programs, is applications oriented—and not only toward the equipment and the software. Tests and analytical functions are performed on intelligent terminal services, node services, and classic telephone services. Furthermore, an *optimizer* available on-line allocates resources as failures occur.

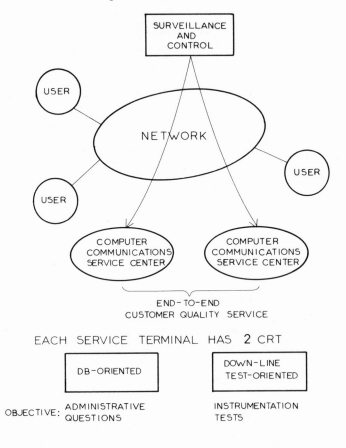

Figure 15.3
Datapac network service center

SURVEILLANCE
AND
CONTROL

USER

NETWORK

USER

USER

COMPUTER
COMMUNICATIONS
SERVICE CENTER

COMPUTER
COMMUNICATIONS
SERVICE CENTER

END-TO-END
CUSTOMER QUALITY SERVICE

EACH SERVICE TERMINAL HAS 2 CRT

DB-ORIENTED

DOWN-LINE
TEST-ORIENTED

OBJECTIVE: ADMINISTRATIVE
QUESTIONS

INSTRUMENTATION
TESTS

Implementing the Maintenance Architecture

The implementation of a maintenance architecture calls for hardware, software, and procedural solutions.

The hardware requirements are the computers at the network control center, the data base media for the described data collection, storage, and retrieval activity, the input–output and the lines and the modems.

The software requirements may be divided into two classes. The first group is the basics, which include telecommunications software, drivers, downline loading, upline dumping, loopbacks, and supervision software. The second group is the applications, the main object of which is inference by means of the data in the data base. Other applications issues are scheduling, dispatching, failure analyses, and inventory management. Many of these applications-oriented programs lead to or require the construction of simulators.

In the basic software we have included downline loading programs. These are needed for execute, memory checks, and read responses. Another important feature is the static and dynamic testing of modems and terminals. Line monitoring and error statistics are absolutely essential. At the NCC the tester must be presented with historical logs, and should be able to request special failure and problem reports on video.

The reliability of the lines is a major subject in itself. Both dependent failures and the variability of line characteristics must be considered. The major source of dependent failures is the use of old standard equipment. The variability of line reliability characteristics makes impossible the achievement of a true real-time application. This is not an issue which affects only the new generation of networks. If anything, the older star-type networks are more exposed to it.

The Danish Savings Banks have 3,000 terminals grouped through 1,000 terminal concentrators on line. Each time the Danish PPT switches from cable to radio linkages from Copenhagen (where the computer resources are) to Jutland, it throws the transmission system out of synchronization. This requires very elaborate procedures to balance the system again.

All over the world, wherever real-time solutions are used, extreme variability of the line reliability parameter is a disturbing factor. Such variability stems from a number of reasons. First is the tremendous variance in the age of the equipment; typically, the life cycle of telephone equipment is 10 to 20 even 30 years. In addition, an equally broad variation exists in the kinds of technologies used; this problem is related to the preceding one and is aggravated by colossal investments in telephone equipment.* Other reasons are a barely controlled situation in equipment environments, and a well-known variability in error rates. A survey in the United Kingdom, for instance, showed 10^{-4} to 10^{-7} variation, and from 2×10^{-5} on one day to 3×10^{-7} on the next. All this for *no* apparent reason.

It is essential that many of the controls be done not only *centrally* but also in the field through interactive terminals. It is exactly these improvements which result in labor savings and higher quality service. To reach this goal, organizational and technological problems have to be overcome. The organization must change as the network topology and service structure change.

The procedural aspects of reorganization are the most critical. In Datapac, for example, they involve four issues.

The centralized report function: This is responsible for receiving, routing, tracking, and disposition of all customer trouble reports.

The centralized dispatch function: Its authority includes the direction and control of all personnel involved in outside installation, repair, and preventive maintenance activities.

The centralized analysis function: This is responsible for network surveillance, information analysis, customer service studies, and correlation of network and customer service problems.

*Some $130 billion in the United States alone.

The centralized test control function: Its goal is controlling the end-to-end testing and sectionalization of impairments to all data services emanating from and entering the operating area of the service center.

The object of the procedural reorganization is to mechanize as quickly as possible the repetitious test setup and execution functions in order to allow the tester to spend more time in the analysis of test results and the resultant human decision-making function. Emphasis has thus been placed on the mechanization of the test function and the automated access of the testing equipment to customer service, across the board of the function and of the units involved in such tests.

Let us recapitulate. The new procedures provide a paperless test-center operation. The data base of the network control center stores equipment records on each customer's service, history logs, and information on the progress of all outstanding impairments. The system provides a trace of progress on all outstanding troubles, allowing field forces and management to analyze and obtain a picture of all controlled maintenance activity in real time. This is done interactively and is video-based. The on-line system is designed to accommodate three types of user control: centralized testers which can initiate tests; tests initiated by installers or repairmen from remote points in the network and accomplished by calling the system over the network and communicating via a keyboard interactive terminal or via a special hand-held keyboard device; and the history retained by the system of all tests performed and their results for later administrative analysis.

16

Network Diagnostics and Monitoring

The systems solution presented in the preceding chapter is both technical and managerial. As such, it incorporates loopback tests, network element testing, connection tracing, off-line diagnostics, and automatic fault diagnosis. We have also spoken of networking loading, centralized versus distributed network management, and data communication tests. These comprise the component parts of a solution which goes beyond the simple models we have known in the past.

A *loopback test* involves a different philosophy of running a maintenance function than what we are familiar with. The idea is to have every line within a system able to be turned around and sent back to itself, for instance, the terminal to itself, the terminal to the modem, the terminal to the front end, and the terminal to the host. Failures do occur, and we must be able to isolate the location. This is the essence of diagnostic tests.

Data entered from the keyboard pass through the transmit portion of the terminal to the modem interface. The modem's output data flow is connected to the terminal's input or receive section. Test data are then returned through the DTE devices to output printer or CRT display.

In the loopback mode many of the internal electronic circuits of the terminal must be involved and verified. Functions like parity, communications timing, and buffer operations should be included and tested.

Loopback data flow should be inherent in the modem associated with the remote terminal. Ideally, the modem test signal should pass through the entire modulator and then be looped back through the demodulator.

Let us take as an example the way loopback tests may be implemented with lines, modems, and multiplexers. At the line level this involves carrier responsibilities, self-tests on private or leased lines, analog circuit testing of the parameters, of bandwidth, delay, jitter, phase shift and procedures for such tests (including the needed agreements with telephone companies). Primarily at this level there is also protocol testing—emulation, test messages, and control traps—and digital throughput testing—trapping the entire exchange.

Modems require both analog and digital loopback, self-testing methods, and digital circuit testing of the parameters of clock, data timing, controls, delays.

Loopback tests implemented with multiplexers involve high-speed trunk, operational environment, secondary channel, difficulties of trunk testing (such as format, timing, local and remote), and terminal and host interfaces. This last refers to local versus remote loopbacks, timing considerations, bit/byte, independent testing, interface cable problems, and different control settings.

In general, *network element testing* involves different considerations, starting with subsystem isolation versus location diagnostics and working inward versus outware possibilities. Subsystem isolation brings up a second element—procedures. Procedures regard remove and replace, remote switching to alternative modules or subsystems, and centralized versus remote testing environment.

Fault isolation is a good approach by which users can learn how to do their own testing; utilities are also helpful. After identification of the element or board which is not performing, replacement may be done locally since most current board designs are plug-in/plug-out.

Coping with line failures is a little more complex. We must study routing alternatives such as end-to-end; with loading points—queues, percentage idle, percentage of input–output; circuit downs; and retries. The monitoring of failures must include the number of block transmissions, location of circuit downs, and the number of retries.

Connection tracing typically involves forced configuration, traced configuration, point-to-point identification of switched circuits, constant monitoring of pathways, and requirements for load analysis and billing.

Off-line diagnostics pertain both to manual testing (remove and replace, loopbacks, test configuration) and automatic testing (preprogrammed data patterns, network simulators, isolation of suspected subsystem or module).

Loopback tests are the basic ingredient for *automatic fault diagnosis*, which, in turn, must provide for both normal failures and catastrophic ones. If the CPU, the front end, and so on should lose power, an automatic switch line (hot switch) must be able to channel resources to backups. This calls for hardware and software support. The hardware must monitor circuit parameters, detect circuit quality, and conduct tests on throughput, turnaround, and channel operations. Correspondingly, the software should, keep connect statistics, permit remote loopbacks, monitor error detection, and test alternative routing. Terminal and host channels must be tested and a location detection facility provided. The latter should foresee monitoring of error detection and correction, alternative routing selection, and isolation of computer failures.

Finally, network access protection involves access methods including open or closed network, locations of access points, hardware/software methods for invoking network control, and trunk and interface circuits (private dedicated service, switched private or public service). In addition, it entails host and network interface (access check, network control) plus use of network services, more specifically scheduling, billing, loading statistics, and diagnostic services.

Applications with Remote Diagnostics

In this section we shall discuss the line and terminal and host monitoring techniques as applied by two users, Bache Halsey Stuart Shields Inc. and First National Bank of Seattle, and by two manufacturers, Digital Equipment Corporation and Intertel. These exemplify pragmatic approaches and document what needs to be done by the way of implementation.

Bache, one of the largest stockbrokerage firms in the United States, has currently in operation a real-time system, based on two Univac 494,* which has managed a centralized starlike network since the mid-1960s. These machines coordinate worldwide the Bache communications facilities, with a dual minicomputer installed in London for interfacing. However, the system is scheduled to change in order to combine the information systems into one network, aiming to reduce people, cut down hardware costs, extend the life of the software, and unify maintenance.** They also want to make available a growth capability for the next five years, while integrating their files.† Their operations managers have to consult four different volumes of paper to find some information. What they want is to get the information in one shot on the screen from *one* data base, whether centralized or decentralized.

The other important network Bache has is the minicomputer-run configuration for its branch offices. This is most interesting since it is a significant development from a former Telex service. Some 150 branch offices are covered by this network, all former Telex users. There are four to six videos per branch office projecting market information. Another application is under study to include customer information, thus integrating with the real-time applications.

Apart from the videos, the present configuration includes two printers: one for the branch office and the other for the Bache news service. Not only did this approach improve the efficiency of the operation, but it also reduced the costs. Bache referred to a $100,000 cost reduction per year as compared to the teletype operation, and the results, management said, were much better.

Still greater savings would materialize from the projected reduction of paper work through the use of soft copies. Ply-paper alone for computer output costs one million dollars a year.

---

*Scheduled for conversion to IBM 3032.

**There are 6 more computers working batch: two 360/65, and four 360/30. These are scheduled for removal with their functions either being integrated into the new real-time system or being distributed. To make feasible a minimum amount of code rewriting, Bache chose two IBM 3032s as its next system; the IBM programs are compatible, while Univac had no machine whose software would follow up on the 494.

†Bache was quick to underline that the integration of files requires a hard look on the software side.

Figure 16.1

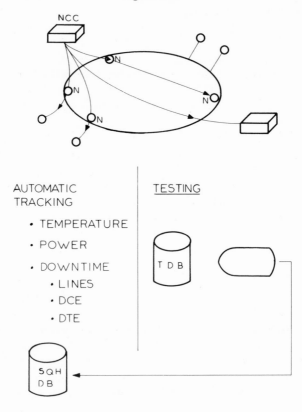

AUTOMATIC
TRACKING

    • TEMPERATURE

    • POWER

    • DOWNTIME

      • LINES

      • DCE

      • DTE

TESTING

The part of Bache's network most relevant to our subject here is the communications control center built to manage the on-line maintenance operations for the aforementioned branch office minicomputers and terminals. The following functions are ensured: control over communications, monitoring of all circuits, failure logging, on-line testing, and maintenance scheduling.

The communications control center is operated by two Incoterm minicomputers (16K internal memory) operating twenty-four hours a day. Another Incoterm minicomputer handles the news-wire fuction at night.

Figure 16.1 illustrates the network control center operation. Data collected during the automatic tracking of the critical performance variables extend over the lines; the DCE and the DTE are stored for later retrieval as the need develops. These statistics on quality history (SQH) are supplemented by a test data base (TDB), a data base in which is stored the results of downline tests.

The network control center works twenty-four hours a day. This is necessary for an operation tuned to round-the-clock use requirements. The network works through the night and prepares receipts at each branch office using a 180 CPS printer. In other words, there is a considerable amount of broadcast traffic run by automatic modems throughout day and night hours. The operation allows all branch offices in the morning to find already compiled the data relative to clients, commodities, margins, name and address confirmation, and stock exchange notices.

Some statistics may help establish the profile of this operation. A large branch office of Bache has about 22,000 customers, 200 executions per day, 370 to 400 inputs per day, and an execution ratio of 60 to 65 percent. The reports the typical branch office receives are divided into three main categories.

Listing of all active customer accounts that have a credit or debit balance: One of the offices stated that there are 200 interrogations per day on behalf of the 40 executives working in that office.

Cash-run activity identification: This report indicates the activity in an account as of a particular date. It has roughly 100 inquires per day. A distinction should be made as to the subject of the report, namely, stocks, bonds or commodities.

Margin status and requirements: Margin status particularly concerns the client's buying power; it is calculated on house requirements, above current stock value.

A new study projects these reports on an interactive basis. This will complete the changeover at Bache, since the firm has been moving from Telex to high-speed network, and on to a distributed information system. It also underscores how dependent the company is on its data network and the precautions to be taken for its maintenance.

To enhance the on-line maintenance capabilities, biweekly meetings are held involving AT&T (for the circuits and the modems), General Telephone and Telegraph (for the minicomputers), Bache communications experts, and branch office people (as users). These meetings are vital, having had a great impact on facing day-to-day problems and, in the more general case, on all data communications use. Among the activities taking place in the course of these meetings are rating of performance, reliability evaluation, extrapolations based on the analysis of the log tape, examination of repetitive problems, review of performance evaluation, statistics by type of problem, type of equipment, type of circuit, and reaction of devices to high duty use.

We shall follow this type of service more accurately with the following examples.

Examination of a typical banking environment is the objective of the next case study. Seattle First National Bank installed a control and diagnostic system that isolates data communications problems remotely. It is part of a dedicated on-line banking system able to diagnose and monitor data communications and data transmission in branches throughout the state.

The network diagnostic control system (and the corresponding modems and support data transmission equipment in each branch) provides the bank with systems control and monitoring for all stations in the bank's on-line network. From the central location the NCC gives the bank a window into its analog and digital communications: it identifies that portion of the system which is malfunctioning and provides the ability to restore operations through alternative facilities.

Besides automatic diagnostic test and control functions, the NCC isolates local problems when they occur. Its automatic scanning feature monitors the bank network, providing on-line diagnosis without operator intervention. Should a failure occur, the system alerts the operator with an audible alarm and a message on the console's screen. The operator can then isolate the problem and, when possible, use restorative features to correct the failure with a minimum of downtime.

Some of the malfunctions at a branch location that are reported to the central system are loss of a data terminal's ready signal, loss of carrier from the central site, and loss of data set ready signal. Based on its diagnostic capabilities, the NCC can then perform such restorative features as dial backup of four-wire telephone lines, hot transfer for all remote modems upon command, and modem streaming detection and disabling.

The equipment consists of a microprocessor-oriented diagnostic and control system that operates out of the main channel bank. It allows off-line testing and on-line telemetry functions by scanning all lines and modems on a continuing basis. At the Seattle office the NCC addresses and monitors modems of 2,400 bits per second at each branch, along with multipoint diagnostic master units. The latter operate in conjunction with each modem and permit the diagnostic, monitoring, and restorative features of the system.

The most recent Digital Equipment Corporation, DEC, application is at the remote diagnostic level. To be able to use remote diagnosis of system malfunctions—within the 11/70 environment—users have to provide a dedicated voice-grade telephone line and a data access arrangement. (There are currently about 850 users under the service contract, out of the total 2,000 PDP-11/70 users.)

The remote computerized diagnosis system is composed of three elements.

Electronic console: A microprocessor-controlled unit that performs system diagnostic procedures and communicates with the remote host computer.

Service response line: A 24-hour toll-free telephone service that makes the initial determination of whether to attempt remote diagnosis.

Digital diagnosis center: The place where the host computer communications equipment and the engineering staff are located.

The electronic console is used in place of the regular PDP-11/70 front panel, allowing users to initiate operating commands through the system terminal. When a system malfunctions, the user dials the toll-free number to contact the service response group, which then arranges for remote diagnosis and reaches the appropriate field service office to schedule a service call. Configuration files are used to determine proper parameters and diagnostic procedures for specific systems. The console also allows the remote host system to log problems for each installation so trends may be identified and flagged.

The above-mentioned system is projected, operated, and maintained by DEC, but NCC systems are now being offered to the ultimate user for proprietary operation. An example is Intertel's fully automated diagnostic and control system able to follow up 160 lines and 6,400 drops of data networks. Such networks may contain point-to-point, multipoint, and multiplexed transmission facilities, and distributed processors. Most combinations of four-wire transmission facilities can be serviced.

Intertel's system has four operating modes.

In the first, automatic network configuration learning (self-learn), a processor at the central site can query the system automatically, learn its configuration, and build a directory without operator intervention.

With background monitoring or automatic monitoring, AM, the system can operate on an unattended basis, checking continually the status of all lines and drops in the network to determine what changes are taking place. Scanning of a network with 10 lines and 20 drops per line occurs in less than 60 seconds. In pinpointing problems, the system makes diagnoses based on events or status changes then displays full details in English with data recorded simultaneously as a printout.

The third mode is automatic predictive maintenance, APM. The system is user programmed to automatically initiate on- and off-line in-depth testing at specific times of the day. Results are recorded by the printer, allowing completely unattended operation during off-hours. Hard-copy records may be used as an indicator of trends in equipment performances for predictive failure analysis.

In a comprehensive, manually initiated test and control mode, the user initiates a test directly by keystrokes on the console keyboard. Results are shown on the console display and may be recorded by the printer.

The architecture, like that of a distributed system has three types of processors: central (CP), satellite (SP), and remote test (RTP). Keeping processing as close to the source data as possible improves data transmission efficiencies and speeds.

The controller is based on a firmware-driven, multiple-processor design. The central controller consists of a CP connected to a system bus. Operator input–output devices connect directly to the CP through serial interface ports.

Also connected to the system bus are multiple SPs, which control operations in self-learn and AM modes and also serve as interface to the user's network. Each SP behaves much like a front-end processor, and is responsible for inquiry–response polling of all RTPs connected directly or indirectly over telephone lines to its ports.

The RTP continuously performs fourteen tests at each remote drop to accomplish status check. Polling of all lines occurs simultaneously in parallel. Thus, the longest time to scan a network is governed by the line with the most drops, not by the number of lines.

Primary system interface is through an operator console from which operations for all ports, lines, and drops can be controlled. It comprises a keyboard and display. The console together with a record-only printer constitute the work station.

The modular structure, processor power, memory capacity, and input–output support may be upgraded.

Finally, within the last few years specific interest has been focused on local loop arrangements. Indeed, there has been a birth of a new telecommunications industry—specialized common carriers, SCC. These carriers, regulated by the FCC, offer private-line voice and data service, primarily between large urban areas. While the marketing impetus for SCCs has been mainly for voice applications, a cable system can quite easily interface to these analog circuits.

SCCs provide interstate microwave radio channels between central city locations. It is now necessary to connect the microwave radios located in a tall building (say, the Empire State) with the customer's location, say, Wall Street. This portion of the circuit, while only a small fraction of the overall circuit mileage, comprises the telecommunications manager's nightmare—the local loop; it is this section of the circuit that tends to cause a majority of the recorded outages.

Presently, the Bell System provides these local loops for the SCCs, probably at an economic loss because of the amount of maintenance required. There are many requests for increased tariffs for these loops by Bell System companies operating across the country.

While it might be uneconomical for a cable television company to provide a single loop between microwave hub and customer, it would seem quite possible and plausible for a cable system to provide loops for multichannel customers or those with broadband requirements. An example could be local interconnection of a broadcast studio to the ultimate user.

User-operated local loops* create many maintenance problems which the general industrial and trading company is simply not equipped to handle. Here again, computer-run, on-line maintenance procedures—able to hookup to professional maintenance operators—seem to have a bright future.

A Case Study with the Danish Savings Banks

On-line maintenance on a limited scale, gaining the maximum advantage of the resources available for processing purposes, is exemplified in an application by the Danish Savings Banks. This teleprocessing and data processing application encompasses 1,000 branch offices; an equal number of terminal concentrators and data collection if maxicomputers or lines are down (with a one-cassette capability for local journaling); a concentrator which can handle up to six terminals, and is programmed to handle format control, check digit, and so on; 3,000 teller terminals, roughly 80 percent at the windows and 20 percent in back-office operation, each with a mini-video display, hard copy, keyboard, and passbook device.

An average of 700,000 transactions are handled on-line per day. The maximum has been 1,520,000 on-line transactions in one long workday. The normal work load is augmented by some 300,000 clearance and other items to the one million

---

*Over the years, local loops have been a weak spot. Those belonging to telephone companies have usually been poorly serviced because of a lack of competition.

Figure 16.2

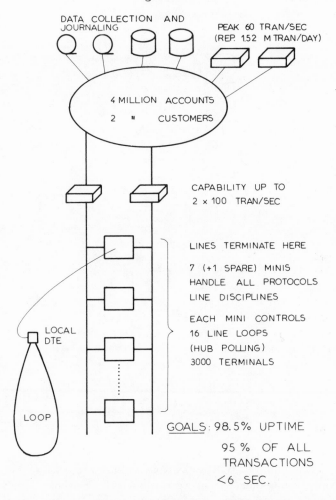

DATA COLLECTION AND JOURNALING

PEAK 60 TRAN/SEC
(REP. 152 M TRAN/DAY)

4 MILLION ACCOUNTS
2 " CUSTOMERS

CAPABILITY UP TO
2 × 100 TRAN/SEC

LOCAL DTE

LINES TERMINATE HERE

7 (+1 SPARE) MINIS
HANDLE ALL PROTOCOLS
LINE DISCIPLINES

EACH MINI CONTROLS
16 LINE LOOPS
(HUB POLLING)
3000 TERMINALS

LOOP

GOALS: 98.5% UPTIME

95 % OF ALL
TRANSACTIONS
<6 SEC.

per day level. The system handles on-line a total of three million central information file names—of which a little over two million are distinct customer entities. (The balance is accounted for by area and bank variations.) Including clients, there are slightly less than four million accounts.

Two maxicomputers handle the traffic and batch operations (IBM 168 and 158, of which one is scheduled to change to Amdhal). Each of the front ends, done by Collins, is capable of handling 100 transactions per second (2 × 100). The mainframe handles roughly 70 transactions per second; the current peak is 60 transactions per second. Loop management is also done by Collins; see Figure 16.2. Each controls up to 16 line loops. Some 90 loops run the aforementioned 3,000 terminals. Hub polling is the discipline being used. The same principle is applied in the maxicomputer and front end loop.

Figure 16.3

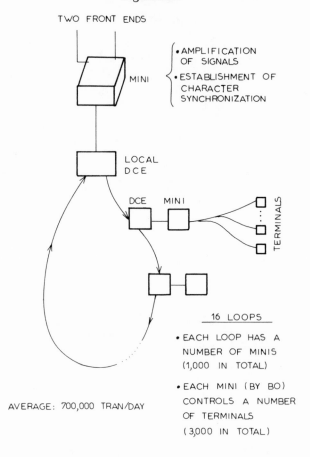

TWO FRONT ENDS

MINI

- AMPLIFICATION OF SIGNALS
- ESTABLISHMENT OF CHARACTER SYNCHRONIZATION

LOCAL DCE

DCE   MINI

TERMINALS

16 LOOPS

- EACH LOOP HAS A NUMBER OF MINIS (1,000 IN TOTAL)
- EACH MINI (BY BO) CONTROLS A NUMBER OF TERMINALS (3,000 IN TOTAL)

AVERAGE: 700,000 TRAN/DAY

The telecommunications network involves 40,000 kilometers of leased lines at a cost of about one million dollars per year with only 0.5 percent time out. The total system strives for 98.5 percent uptime, 95 percent of all transactions to have delays of less than six seconds (all sorts included), and about two transactions per terminal per minute at peak time.

The applications are divided into thirty subsystems: 90 percent of the programs are common to all banks, 10 percent are dedicated. As the application evolves, the object is to integrate user subsystems; current accounts, savings, and loans are the first ones chosen for integration.

The terminal concentrators, too, will change. The specifications being considered call for ten-megabyte discs at the minicomputer, one type of teller terminals, two types of back-office terminals, inquiry capability, and ability to handle automatic teller machines.

The maintenance application is as follows: All terminals are mapped on a panel located in the control room. Data is fed to the panel by each PDP for the loops which it controls; see Figure 16.3. The status of the loops and of the concentrators is indicated. Failure of a loop activates an immediate reaction from the centralized control room towards the PTT (a direct, private line has been installed for this purpose). Failure of a terminal concentrator calls for corrective action on behalf of the manufacturer. In both failures the need for repetitive (and often inefficient) telephone calls between the branch office and the center has been eliminated. Delays are nonexistent.

At the central location, the modems interface with the PDP via printed circuit board with test capability. This front end also handles amplification of signals and establishment of character synchronization. If character synchronization is assured, the lights are switched off the map. If not, the lights are on, bringing the controller's attention to a deficiency. This is one of the major problems of all on-line installations; telephone companies often switch between, say, coaxial and radio links, without informing the client—and synchronization has to be re-established within seconds.

Though the prevailing protocol is hub polling, front ends can be programmed to handle any line discipline. Indeed, in this particular solution, the external loop concentrators incorporate a fairly extensive ability for acting as gateways.

Index

Page numbers in *italics* indicate material
contained in figures and tables.